Riding in Cars with Dogs

because cats don't travel well

a memoir

Julie Ann

 BOOK SMART

Book Smart
Nashville, TN

ISBN: 979-8-9919435-0-5

Library of Congress Control Number: 2024924149

For Elsa
Ginger
Kippy
&
Baby
(Shakespeare, too)

The greatness of a nation and its moral progress
can be judged by the way its animals are treated.

—Mahatma Gandhi

This is a memoir from my point of view that focuses on my life with animals, not a comprehensive autobiography that covers all my life's events. Some human names have been changed, but animal names—living, dead, real, or stuffed—have not (they all gave permission telepathically). While I have done my best to present my recollections as accurately as possible, memory is a funny thing. Capturing how I felt twenty or thirty years ago is suspect no matter how good the memory. no matter how many diaries kept, and no matter how many pictures consulted for details. Others can write their own versions—I would be especially intrigued to read my pets' memoirs, if only they could type.

ALL PETS WELCOME

D*oggie*: The first word I ever spoke, even though we didn't own a dog. In my baby book under my First Year Likes, Mom wrote *animals* along with *bananas* and *TV commercials*.

My love of animals is configured in my DNA, much like my blue eyes or my flat hair. I was born with an obsessive adoration for the cuteness that kitties and puppies and bunnies and squirrels possess. Whether real or stuffed or on television screens or in picture books, animals drew me to them like a lovelorn Montague to an ambivalent Capulet.

Animals dictate my world although I am not a farmer or breeder or zoologist. A lover, an admirer is all I am for I figured out the secret, probably when I toddled around babbling *doggie*. The world is a much cuter place, a more forgiving place, and a less egocentric place when we share our space with animals, when we care for them and they care for us. (They may also chew up mopboards, destroy carpets, whine incessantly, pout, demand attention, and occasionally cause allergic reactions.) Animals teach us vital

life lessons, lessons only they can impart.
Calling me an animal lover is an understatement.

MAN IS IN THE FOREST

My first animal memory: watching *Bambi*.

I giggled at Thumper as his leg thumped up and down and at Bambi as he tried to ice skate on his spindly legs. The magical forest with its adorable animals marked itself as my first movie memory. The exploding gunshot, deer running, fear in their almond-shaped eyes shattered all fairy-tale tranquility. When Bambi asked his mom why they ran, she said, "Man was in the forest." Later in the movie, another gunshot. This one executed Bambi's mother.

From an early age, I knew I would never marry a man who hunted. "Man was in the forest" carved itself into my soul with the image of Bambi's big eyes filling with tears. Thanks to *Bambi*, I panicked every time an animal appeared in a movie, overwhelmed with the possibility that the furry little creature may not make it to the end, that man was lurking in the forest.

Alien: Mom sent me and Sister, older than me by four years, out of the room when the alien popped through Kane's stomach, a scene I wouldn't see until junior high. *Alien* was not a family movie we watched together, but rather one of those left on HBO while Sister and I entertained ourselves. In the early Eighties, HBO only played R-rated movies at night, so I never saw much of the movie if it started past seven o'clock. Mom must not have thought the alien would scare us. The square-shaped, long-legged, salivating toothy monster didn't interest me, only the cat caught my attention. I knew some slimy alien was killing off characters, nameless people to me who all looked grimy and similar in the darkness of the spaceship. But Jonesy the cat must survive to the end. I said, "Where's the cat? She has to find the cat." Dad said, "The dumb broad." I didn't think Ripley was dumb for trying to find the cat, only that she was dumb because she had the cat and then she let it run away again.

The Tale of Peter Rabbit: I loathed Mr. McGregor. I didn't care if he died.

The Velveteen Rabbit: Stuffed or real, the line blurred for me because my stuffed animals *were* real. They had feelings and hopes and dreams just like everyone. I had scarlet fever when I was six and suffered from nightmares about my stuffed animals burning to death like in the story. *The Velveteen Rabbit* was the first book that made me cry, especially the part when he thought the little boy had abandoned him.

Old Yeller: Who thinks up such shit? *Old Yeller* is the most indefensible story for little kids. What lesson does it teach us? That we must make tough decisions and shoot our pets? I'm surprised this story has survived, considering it places a gun in a child's hand. I would draw parallels to *Old Yeller* when I read *Of Mice and Men* in high school. Curiously, *Of Mice and Men* became one of my favorite books.

Charlotte's Web: Couldn't get past the whole spider thing. When is a spider not a demonic bug sent to terrorize us? (I know spiders aren't bugs, but they are still demons.)

The Lost Boys: *The Lost Boys* became my favorite movie (even slightly ahead of *Dirty Dancing*, *The Legend of Billie Jean*, and *Heathers*). Sexy vampires, a girl named Star with Barbie-like hair who wore glittery bohemian skirts, and—the best part—Nanook, the astute husky who pushed one of the vampires into the bathtub full of holy water and garlic. Nanook survived heroic and unscathed. The scene that solidified my favoritism: when Sam and Michael raced outside to save Nanook from the incoming vampires.

The Lion King: Despite my high school stubbornness, I accompanied a friend to the theater to see *The Lion King*. Everyone raved about it, but I didn't understand the draw of a Disney movie for teenagers or childless adults. *The Lion King* revealed all that was wrong with Disney as I compared it to *Bambi*, although I felt detached from the father lion (more on that later). After *The Lion King*, I swore never to watch a Disney movie again with animals as characters. *Toy Story* and *Shrek* were the only animated movies I watched until my son was born. He wasn't fond of watching movies, so I saw only a handful: *The Bee Movie*, *Ice Age*, *The Secret*

Life of Pets, and *Cars*. All animals survived (although a car may not have).

Turner and Hooch: Never watched it. I assumed correctly that Hooch would not survive in the end.

Con Air: I admit to keeping track of the stuffed bunny.

Marley & Me: Tempting, but after about 30 minutes, I abandoned it, leaving Marley in a perpetual state of Not Dead Yet.

I Am Legend: I knew it. I shouldn't have watched it.

Dewey: The Small-Town Library Cat Who Touched the World: I read this for a neighborhood mom book club. I prepared myself, knowing that the cat wouldn't live forever. I couldn't understand, even as a 35-year-old woman, why every library didn't have a cat.

Hachi: My fellow teacher selected this movie for our juvenile detention students to watch one holiday. I attempted to hide my tears, even stepping into my office toward the end of the movie to wipe my eyes before my mascara smeared. Because it was a true story, I was more accepting of its tragic end. In fiction, why would one ever choose to end a pet's life?

"Traveling Through the Dark" by William E. Stafford is the poem I love to hate. Why didn't the narrator call 911 to save the unborn baby deer? I imagine myself—despite my fainting problem—as Dr. Lewis on *ER*, out in the field, turning a pen into a surgical device and saving the fawn.

The Walking Dead: I should have stopped watching after Glenn died (especially how they killed him), but when Dog appeared, I now had someone to worry about, as I had become jaded with the remaining characters and repetitious storyline. At least Dog survived to the finale.

"The Otters and the Seaweed" by Teddy Macker—don't Google this poem if you treasure a good night's sleep. Images of otters waking up in the middle of the night in the middle of the ocean, alone, floating, lost forever, flashed behind my eyelids, taunting me as I yearned for sleep. I couldn't shake my melancholy for days. Why must nature be so cruel?

Even innocuous Emily Dickinson has faced my wrath. I adore her, even more than Sylvia Plath, for her introverted reclusive ways who did her own thing and told the rest of the world to fuck off. A couple of biographies—lengthy, four-hundred-page ones—described her drowning kittens in vinegar. Emily was not quite so dear to me anymore.

No, I don't place animals above humans. My mascara threatens to run every time I watch *Steel Magnolias* and *Legends of the Fall* and the episode of *Little House on the Prairie* when the blind school burns down. And let's not forget Glenn. Perhaps I've accepted human mortality. I know I will die someday. For whatever reason, I have not accepted that my dog or cat will die someday.

FAIRY TAILS AND BARBIE DOGS

My childhood world consisted of princesses and crowns, everything pink, dresses and fairy tales, and puppies and kitties and bunny rabbits and birds and deer and squirrels and chipmunks... I gravitated to animals rather than people, preferring to sit and pet a cat than to interact with someone my age.

Even at four years old, I analyzed everything ad nauseum. If I didn't care about something, it ceased to matter to me even in the face of peer pressure. But if something caught my attention, I critiqued it even if I didn't possess the vocabulary to adequately express my opinion.

Fairy tales are not created equally.

Snow White was the first I remember, a huge storybook filled with pictures of the princess dancing with the Dwarves and kissing the Prince. I wasn't fond of Snow White's short hair nor her clown-like dress, although I adored her heels with the bow. The creepy Seven Dwarves might as well have been related to Rumpelstiltskin. The nameless Prince shows up out of nowhere. The end. Wasn't a fan.

Cinderella annoyed me. How could someone be sad sewing with mice and birds? I would have given anything for birds to fly through my window and help me sew a pretty pink dress, which I preferred over the Fairy Godmother dress Cinderella is known for wearing. Then Prince Charming, who is anything but charming, searches door to door to find the woman of his dreams, with only a shoe to differentiate her from the slovenly girls. Shouldn't he recognize her face, or at least her eyes? Technically the Cinderella he's searching for doesn't exist. Her authentic self is the one who's depressed and finds no joy sewing with birds and mice—a Cinderella Prince Charming would never find attractive. Prince Charming doesn't even look for his dream woman by himself; he's rude to his nameless sidekick. Prince Charming is wimpy and entitled. Cinderella is fake. Not a fan, although I loved the idea of glass slippers, fairy godmothers, pumpkin-shaped carriages, and fancy ballgowns.

Sleeping Beauty was my favorite. Prince Philip falls in love with Princess Aurora while she's in the forest dancing and singing with her animal friends. She's lonely but makes the best of it. Prince Philip is kind to his horse, Samson, whom he treats like a beloved family member. It ends with Prince Philip's kiss waking Sleeping Beauty from her slumber. Plus, the OG Sleeping Beauty wears a blue dress, not the pink one of every merchandiser. For some reason, Mom always dressed me in blue despite my declaration that I wanted everything pink. Sure, Sleeping Beauty is on screen for the least amount of time of any princess, barely speaks any lines, doesn't follow directions, and relies on Prince Philip to rescue her. But it's the animals and Sleeping

Beauty's interaction with them that enchanted me the most (and all the animals survive, including Samson).

I longed to be Sleeping Beauty.

I channeled such dreams into my Barbies and their lives.

My Barbies didn't have babies—they had pets. It all started with Beauty, the 1979 Afghan hound. I don't remember receiving her, only that she was there alongside Golden Dream Barbie. The first Barbie I remember getting was Roller Skating Barbie for Christmas in 1981, yet Beauty and Golden Dream Barbie existed before that memory.

For my sister's eighth birthday, my parents bought her the yellow Corvette. I would have the pink Corvette a couple of years later (then the silver one, then the metallic magenta one, and finally the '57 Chevy, which was the most fun for its backseat and large trunk). Barbie drove around with her friends, both doll and stuffed, but she preferred taking Beauty along. (Ken had plastic hair at the time and Sister and I found him unappealing, especially when we desired the hair of Rick Springfield and Duran Duran on our future husbands, so we never owned a Ken.) If I positioned Beauty just right, I could buckle her in using the plastic shoulder strap seatbelt.

Barbie's pet collection grew: Sister got Dallas (to go with her Western Barbie), then I got Dallas's baby, Dixie. Then Sister got Fluff, the cat, whom I desperately wanted, but I ended up with Prancer, the white Arabian horse, and lastly Prince, the French poodle who wore a raspberry-colored beret, a song I knew well. Sometimes I squeezed both Prince and Beauty into the passenger seat, with Fluff in his carrier on the floor. Before support animals were a thing, Barbie frequently shopped and traveled with her animal entourage, stopping at McDonald's on their way home (all pets received their own hamburger, bun included).

That's how I imagined my life as an adult: I'd drive around in a convertible (not necessarily a Corvette), preferably a pink one, with my dogs and cats to visit the stables where the likes of Prancer, Dixie, and Dallas awaited our arrival. After stopping for some lunch, I would return home to play in my backyard with my dogs and cats and dance around with squirrels and bunnies and birds. Just like Sleeping Beauty.

HAROLD (#1 & #2)

My parents often spoke of their childhood animals. Without a dog or a cat to call my own, I was envious of their animal friends.

Dad told stories about Fred the cat who could open doors. Mom had a little terrier, Scamp, who appeared in a myriad of childhood pictures, who would run to the piano and howl to "They Call the Wind Maria" whenever Mom played it. I envisioned a new childhood for myself, one where I had a lap dog or a kitty who followed me everywhere.

Both my parents grew up on farms, so cats were abundant and stray dogs came and went. Mom even had a pony named Lady. Some of my favorite pictures of my parents before they were parents involved raccoons. While they were dating in high school, Dad found baby raccoons on his farm and gave them to Mom to raise, as she had bred bunnies and guinea pigs and knew how to care for orphaned wild babies. In one picture, Mom cradled a raccoon like a baby and bottle fed it. In another, a much larger raccoon

13

played with Dad's hair from the back of the couch. Another raccoon posed with a pink bow on his head.

That is how I imagined Sleeping Beauty's life. It's the life I wanted.

The closest I came to a fairy-tale forest was Grandpa C's farm, the same farm of Mom's childhood. It provided the only place for real animals: tons of stray cats and Benji. But neither fulfilled my I-want-to-carry-you-around-all-day-long pet dream.

Grandpa kept Benji in a pen outside, which connected to a large shed, like a mansion-sized doghouse. A stocky black lab, Benji was not the snuggle puppy I desired. Sister and I always helped Grandpa with his morning chores when we visited: we fed and watered Benji while Grandpa cleaned up the poop. Benji joined us while we walked the acreage, zooming around with his freedom: he'd stampede in one direction, back to us, then dart off in the other direction. Although his antics gave me the giggles, he was much too big and wild for me. His coarse hair wasn't snuggleable either.

We could rarely catch the farm cats—they wanted no part of snuggling. None were allowed in the house, no matter how much I begged. I was more drawn to the kittens, most of them black, maybe a few tabbies and calicos, but they were all wild, only congregating when Grandpa fed them. Mom hollered at us before we went outside, "Stay away from the gooey-eyed ones." Those were the only ones we could catch.

Sister was older and braver than me, so she'd snatch a kitten from the ground and place it in the metal stroller I had prepared just for the occasion. I couldn't walk more than two steps before the cat bailed, jumping out and running far away from the needy girls who wanted to treat them like baby dolls.

Such instances could not assuage my longing for a real live cuddle pet.

Enter Harold.

I don't remember how Harold came to be. I was barely four years old. Mom budgeted every penny we had, but somehow, perhaps through our begging, we ended up with a hamster.

A cantankerous hamster who scratched and bit and wiggled who wanted no part of snuggling.

I remember little about Harold, only that Dad set his cage as far from the bedrooms as possible since Harold liked to exercise on his wheel in the middle of the night. Dad couldn't sleep with a ticking clock, so a squeaky hamster wheel must be silenced. Because of Harold's midnight boot camp, he slept during the day. I thought that would make him more snuggly, but it only made him madder when I plucked him from the plastic cup that was his bed during his all-day slumber. Once he bit me, I never held him again.

Harold ran away. Or something. I don't know the circumstances of his disappearance.

Enter Harold #2. (Or maybe I never knew Harold #1, only that Harold #2 was in fact our second hamster. The details matter little.)

Harold #2 survived our move all the way from Iowa to Utah only to die a couple months later. Using an old-fashioned crayon box as a coffin, Mom or Dad placed Harold's furry body inside it. We probably put a blanket or a piece of fabric in there with him. I imagine setting a dandelion beside him because it sounds like something I would have done. We buried him in our garden. I was sad that he was gone, but I didn't know him that well, with the lack of snuggling and all.

Even a hamster—a Scrooge-like one—alters the household chemistry with its presence. A palpable emptiness lingered in the space of Harold's cage.

As an adult during the Beanie Baby craze, I stumbled upon a hamster who looked just like Harold (and all other hamsters in the world). He was one of the few stuffed animals I kept as an adult. He doesn't bite.

A KITTY CAT INTERLUDE

Every crayon picture I drew of a house, a kitty sat in the window. My crude drawing of a cat only contained geometric shapes: circles for the head and body, triangles for the ears, and thin rectangles for the legs. I even added cats to the houses in coloring books. Because what house wouldn't have a cat sleeping in the window?

My grandparents' houses provided my only fix for my cat addiction, albeit brief.

Grandpa C befriended a full-grown yellow cat, one that showed up on his porch one day, carrying himself as a city cat with the well-to-do of a housecat. He didn't have a name, just Yellow Cat. Grandpa let Yellow Cat inside the house. Yellow Cat lasted only one of our visits—his whereabouts remained unknown.

At my paternal grandparents' house in town, a stray gray cat hung around the yard, so Grandma J fed it. We called him Gray. The adults in my family were not known for their creative names.

Before we moved to Utah when I was four, we spent a

couple of months living with my grandparents. Gray was tame, friendly, and sat in my lap for short amounts of time, the closest I came to having a cat for a pet. Before we moved, Mom took a picture of me, Sister, and Dad holding Gray. By the time we visited at Christmas, Gray was long gone.

Not that I didn't love dogs. There was just something about a cat, especially those dressed in sweaters and hats or Christmas vintage ones poking their heads out of decorative boxes adorned with bows. I cherished my porcelain Dime Store figurines, a momma and her two kittens, that I bought using Grandpa C's dimes, nickels, and quarters he always saved for us. They must have been made of some sort of spacecraft porcelain for they never broke no matter how many times I dropped them. Their little tails and ears remain intact without a chip on them.

I had to remain content with coloring cats into windows and admiring my porcelain ones, for a cat would never be part of my childhood.

HELLO, MIKEY

Mikey, our first family dog, appeared from nowhere, as if a stork had dropped him from the sky over our house one late fall day when I was four years old.

(In actuality, one of our neighbors in Salt Lake City had a collie. She disappeared into the mountains and was pregnant upon her return. We ended up with one of the male pups.)

How we settled upon Mikey as his name, I have no idea. And apparently I have spelled his name incorrectly my entire life. On the back of Mikey's pictures, Mom, in her perfect left-handed cursive writing, spelled his name *M-i-k-e*. Perhaps I didn't understand that the *e* didn't always have to be silent. I cannot change my ways now, so I will forever spell his name with a *y*.

When Sister and I first met Mikey, he fell asleep. Sister placed the little furball into her pink plastic baby doll bathtub. I fetched my light-yellow baby blanket, which Sister folded to fit the bathtub, then covered the now sleeping puppy. Mom took our picture together. I'm beaming as if the new puppy is a miracle, a panacea for all the sadness in the world.

Mikey looked more like a light brown German shepherd than a collie. His long black snout topped a sandy brown body covered in soft, short fur. As he aged, his ears and tail sprouted fluffy brown fur like a collie, yet his legs grew tall and long, his slender body like that of a wolf.

Mom reminded me daily, "Puppies spend a lot of time sleeping." My lower lip stuck out as Mikey napped incessantly. I always searched for his whereabouts, wanting to know his location just in case he woke up and wanted to cuddle or play (or better yet, let me carry him around all day long). My idea of playing consisted of rolling around on the floor with him or running around the house, probably chasing after him more than he chased after me.

Watching Dad play with Mikey was more fun than watching *The Dukes of Hazzard*. When Mikey laid on his back, Dad turned a back paw into a stick shift, adding sound effects as he shifted Mikey's leg. Mikey responded by batting his paws around, squirming on the carpet as Dad slammed his hand to the floor. Mikey sprang to his feet and ran around the house in circles, always returning for more, plopping down on his back in front of Dad for another round. I begged Dad to do that again and again as I squealed while Mikey ran in zigzags. Even when he wasn't fraught with hyper-puppiness, Mikey would run headfirst into our white freezer.

Mom sent cassette tapes back to my grandparents in Iowa, for that was cheaper than paying for long-distance phone calls (a concept younger generations will never comprehend). She said of our new puppy: "Julie has developed quite a bond with Mikey. She feeds him from the table and always lets him in and out. It's really rather cute to watch." Her voice relays such sweetness to my grandparents, a sentimental tone Mom reserved only for the most special circumstances.

Mikey was the first in a long line of animals I loved feeding from the table.

As homebodies, we spent our evenings gathered around the television set. Sister and I lounged on the floor in front of the TV, dragging Mom-made pillows from the couch. Mikey joined us, resting his big snout on my pillow or rooting around in our blankets to plop between us.

Like all pets everywhere, Mikey loved jumping on beds when we washed the sheets. All pets find an exposed mattress fun and fascinating. They also think it's grand to position themselves between the sheet and the mattress as you try to remake the bed with sheets that just came off the clothesline (it was the early Eighties, so we didn't use our dryer that often). Mikey pounced on the bed as if ready to attack, thinking it was playtime rather than make-the-bed time. I giggled while I attempted to shoo him from my bed, a welcome distraction on our cleaning Mondays.

Mikey slept in our garage but was an indoor-outdoor dog. My first instinct as I write this forty years after Mikey's birth was that he was not allowed on the furniture and was promptly booted off as his puppy brain learned appropriate behavior. But I found Polaroids that prove me wrong of a resting puppy on our tweed, striped-brown couch with his head up against the arm pillow. Mom sat on the other end of the couch cross-stitching, fully aware of Mikey's infraction, which must not have been against the rules.

By the time Mom took a picture of Dad, Sister, Mikey, and me in front of our first ever new car—a cream-colored 1981 Thunderbird—Mikey towered over me as we sat together, the perfect height for bear hugs, which I subjected him to multiple times a day. The scenic mountains in the background archive our only year in Utah.

I have little memory of moving from Salt Lake City to South Dakota, only that Mikey came with us, and moved with us again from our rental to our first owned home. He still slept in the garage as before. When my grandparents visited us, Dad and Grandpa J constructed a doghouse for Mikey and painted it white. The doghouse sat on our big concrete patio behind the garage. Our huge, fenced-in yard was perfect for Mikey.

That yard would become Mikey's undoing.

STUFFED REALITIES

Despite the blue paint on the walls and the multi-tone blue shag carpeting on the floor, my room was a utopia.

Mom bordered the wall with stenciled puppies and hearts she painted dark blue. My homemade pink quilt gave my room its only splash of my favorite color. From one corner of the wall to the next, I hung animal posters, the ones found in school book orders. White fluffy kittens and cocker spaniel puppies hung alongside ponies and chickens and zebras and tiger cubs. Because my Barbie stuff took up so much space in my closet, my huge pile of stuffed animals filled one corner of my room.

I collected stuffed animals, having almost one hundred by the time I started counting, and close to four hundred by the time I stopped counting. Everyone bought me stuffed animals for Christmas or Easter or my birthday. Flash from *The Dukes of Hazzard*, Garfield, and Gizmo littered my room, mixed in with all the non-celebrity animals, like Lamby and Ducky and Rabbit and Panda. I saved up my allowance to buy even more stuffed animals.

We rarely went shopping. Mom ran all her errands while Sister and I were at school. Summer offered the best opportunity to adopt more animals. The act of purchasing one brought me equal parts excitement and anxiety as I selected one off the shelf, then put it back, so I could dig around to find the one with the cutest face or the craziest face or, better yet, the one who spoke to me. I apologized to all the others for not choosing them to come home with me—telepathically, since I had the power to mentally transmit messages to all stuffed animals—and guaranteed them that all would find a new home. (As an adult, I still find the one that speaks to me. One Christmas, I fell in love with a decorative festive llama. I bought the one who had a bent ear, giving him a more misfit personality than the rest. I no longer apologize to the others, although on some subconscious level I wonder where the rest will find homes.)

Garage sales were more challenging for me. Mangy, once-loved, now abandoned and neglected scruffy stuffed animals sat haphazardly in cardboard boxes or tables, suddenly homeless, begging to find a new forever home. I saved up all my change for the sole purpose of rescuing as many of these sad animals as possible. (I still grimace when I see a huge stuffed bear strapped to the front of a garbage truck. I doubt the animal is enjoying himself although the alternative would have been the landfill.)

At just six years old, I had already decided on my Miss America platform: to save every dog and cat on the planet. But at my young age, I focused my energy on making the stuffed animal world a happy one—World Peace for Plushies.

My stuffed animals served many social purposes for me: they were my well-behaved classroom students, board game contestants, Christmas carolers, library patrons, and sleepover friends. They acted in the holiday play I wrote, although they never performed it for an audience since no human wanted to sit through my creation that I had worked on for weeks. My stuffed animals even recreated "We Are the World," as I matched each animal to their singer, but I had to sing it from memory since we didn't own the record (thankfully MTV played it nonstop). Sunglasses adorned the animals that were Stevie Wonder, Ray Charles, and Michael Jackson; my charm necklace hung from Cyndi Lauper's neck. Earmuffs covered the bigger animals' ears to act as headphones. Whichever animal sang Lionel Richie's part always gave a thumbs up at the end (more like a paw up, as none of my stuffed animals had thumbs).

My favorite (I never admitted to having favorites though) prior to the birth of Care Bears was Little Animal. Mom told me the story of Little Animal because I was too little to remember.

During my early childhood days, we had only one vehicle. Mom stayed home with me, Sister either walked or rode the bus to school, and Dad drove the car to work. Once a month, Mom drove Dad to work. She spent the entire day running errands. That included grocery shopping, anything that wasn't grocery shopping (these were the days before Walmart existed in Iowa), bill paying, bank going, and potentially even stops at the courthouse or DMV. That could make for a long day for a toddler like me.

Having been trained well, I doubt I fussed much anyway. But on this particular day, all the errands had

even exhausted Mom. At our last stop, I picked a miniature stuffed animal off the shelf, strategically placed low for
little ones like me. He was all of four inches tall with a
beanbag butt. The dark brown fluffy scruff of his squirrel
tail was part of the body (it didn't stick out like a tail) and a
wobbly neck supported his tiny tan head. Dark brown felt
ears stuck out on top of his head. Squirrels are my spirit
animals (I'm also convinced I was a cat in a past life). I'm
sure he spoke to me, like the decorative elephant on that
World Market commercial.

We didn't have much expendable income when I was
little, so earning a special treat would have been unheard of
in those days. We never went without at Christmas, but we
were not spoiled with wasteful crap on shopping trips. At
first, Mom shook her head, took Little Animal out of my
hand, and placed him back on the shelf. I plucked him off
the shelf again. Mom told the story: "I couldn't say no. You
had been so good all day and you held onto Little Animal
so tightly." I can envision myself, walking around the store,
carrying Little Animal like a baby bird in my hand, beaming
from ear to ear.

I'm sure I showed my sister right away after school. A
debate ensued about whether he was in fact a squirrel. We
were pretty sure, but just to be safe, we named him Little
Animal.

Little Animal went everywhere with me. He was pock-
et-sized, but I put him on an invisible leash, checking his
whereabouts often. Because of his minute size, he could
hide anywhere: within the sheets on my bed, at the bottom
of our toy box, or even underneath couches. Once I found
him, usually camouflaged within my stuff animal pile, I'd

remind him not to scare me like that again. Little Animal enjoyed riding along with Barbie in her convertible (he couldn't drive because he couldn't reach the pedal nor see over the steering wheel), eating at Barbie's McDonald's set, and playing hide and seek. He did not like baths or anything with water, horseback riding, or when he lost his little felt tongue or when Sister pulled off his dangling felt nose.

On one summer visit to my grandparents' house when I was six or so, Little Animal accompanied me along with a bag full of other stuffed animals. I don't know what horrible thing I had done to my sister, but on that day she was feeling rather nasty. It's common in older siblings.

Sister, without warning or provocation, grabbed Little Animal and said, "He's mine."

How funny I thought. "Give him back," I said, not overly concerned, but I would feel much better if she didn't have him in a death grip and he was sitting in my hand instead.

Sister shook her head. "No, he's mine."

My chest constricted as all the air left my lungs and my heart beat like a pursued rabbit's. "No, he's not. He's mine. Now give him back."

"You can't prove he's yours."

Oh my god, oh my god, oh my god. "He's mine, now give him back," my shrill voice was barely comprehensible.

Sister smirked. "Make me."

"Mom!" I ran into the kitchen where Mom sat with Grandma J.

Now at DEFCON One, I blurted, "Make Sister give me back Little Animal."

I can only assume my mother was enjoying her adult

time, a rarity for her, especially in the summer. I was now the pesky fly that showed up at the picnic.

Mom didn't even look at us, but said halfheartedly, "Give Julie back her animal."

This is Little Animal, not just some random stuffed animal. My eyes narrowed at my mother, who wasn't even looking at me as she lit another cigarette.

Sister shrugged. "But he's mine."

"No he's not. It's Little Animal." I pointed at him, daring Mom to rescind my legal parentage of Little Animal.

"If you want that animal back," Mom nodded at Little Animal as though he meant nothing, even to the point of why we were fighting over *that* raggedy little thing, "you'll have to give Sister one of your other animals."

"But Little Animal is mine! I shouldn't have to give up one of my other animals to get him back!" *Don't you remember the story of Little Animal?* I stood there, tears coming to my eyes as the snot began to drip from my nose. Sister wore a smile of satisfaction. Even my dad knew the story of Little Animal. My mother had betrayed me.

Mom said again, "You've got plenty of other animals. Trade her one of yours if you want that one back."

I sniffled. Grandma spoke. "Now listen to your mom. You can just trade animals. You girls have plenty between the two of you."

Sister already knew which stuffed animal she wanted, as if she had predicted this outcome. "Gimme the elephant." I had a small, teal elephant with hot pink ears. (Sister always had an affinity for such colors. In high school, her dream car was a teal-colored Firebird with a hot pink streak down the side. I would immediately think of this little elephant and this incident all those years later.)

Have you all gone mad? Don't you know how a trade works? You have to own it before you can trade it. I stood there sniffling, wondering if this topsy turvy world where nothing made sense except nonsense itself belonged in *Alice in Wonderland*. That would make Sister the Mad Hatter, Mom the Queen of Hearts, and Grandma the March Hare.

Sister returned to the kitchen with the elephant. I stared at the elephant, then at Little Animal, who was starting to suffocate in Sister's grip. I didn't want to hurt my elephant's feelings by giving him up, but I didn't have a choice. I telepathically apologized to the elephant and took Little Animal from Sister, hugging him close.

I stomped out of the kitchen. Never again did I bring Little Animal anywhere with me. He stayed in the confines of my room to keep him safe from Little Animal-napping. (The once-coveted teal elephant was discarded without thought back into my stuffed animal pile months later.)

While everyone appeared to understand how much I loved my stuffed animals, they didn't *understand* how much I loved my stuffed animals. To me, they were almost real, hovering on the line between imagination and reality, instilling a magical quality in them that allowed them to exist in both worlds at the same time, just like *Toy Story*, which was still decades in the future. With me they froze so that I could decide what we played and how we played it, but when they had my room to themselves, they lived their own lives.

I stopped bringing stuffed animals to Grandma J's house when Grandpa J threatened to throw Bugs Bunny in the oven. I carried around Mom's old-fashioned Bugs

Bunny with the hard face and the pull string to activate his list of sayings, a string I refused to stop pulling, making him say "Now hug me tight," and "(giggle) You're a cute bunny," and "Heya, take me with you," and "Yikes, I hurt myself" and "Now take it easy," and "(giggle) I like you," and "I love carrots (chew, chew, chew)" with a high-pitched voice that was annoying to all adults everywhere.

Stuffed animals were immortal, pending a natural disaster or nuclear war (or a mean sister and a cranky grandparent). Little Animal survived my childhood and now has a permanent spot in my curio cabinet, where I can see his little tattered face every time I sit in my living room. (And Bugs Bunny sits in an old metal stroller downstairs, far from the oven.)

FISH, FOOD, AND THIRTYSOMETHING

My sheltered, city childhood equated to an oblivion regarding the harsh realities of life and death. As a city kid, I didn't have to pluck feathers from dead chickens or bury dogs that were hit by cars. I remained naïve in my fairy-tale land of immortal animals (minus Bambi's mother).

I avoided nature shows with tigers stalking wildebeest, foxes hunting rabbits, even snakes swallowing mice. I knew on some level a food chain existed, that carnivores ate other animals, and that cows provided meat for human consumption. But I never *thought* about it.

Dad and his brothers trapped animals for their hides and hunted pheasants. A Polaroid taken when I was three of Dad and my uncles with dead pheasants shows how much I hated it. Sister sat on my uncle's lap, smiling in the middle of dead birds. I didn't want to be in the picture, sitting on Dad's knee far away from the murdered pheasants. A leery look resides on my face, a grimace as I turned my head away from the birds. That was the last time I joined them for photos of their kill, although Dad stopped hunting and trapping shortly thereafter.

I refused to acknowledge the reality of dead animals and hunters and trappers and roadkill and meat or where the food on my plate originated.

A fish changed all of that.

Like many households in the 1970s and '80s, we had an aquarium—two, in fact, one smaller than the other. The empty aquariums moved with us to three different houses, but I can't recall any particular fish that swam in them. Our small aquarium housed a tadpole we found in a nearby stream, whom we aptly named Todd. I vaguely remember Todd, more like a science experiment than a pet. Once Todd sprouted legs and lost his tail, we promptly released him back into the wild.

I have no memory of us flushing a dead goldfish down the toilet, nor do I remember having named any of our fish. But I sat watching them swim around the tank, thinking that when I had a fish tank someday, I would decorate the bottom with little houses and sparkling pink rocks.

The first searing memory I have of a fish is the one that ended up on my plate.

I loved fish—with Kraft tartar sauce. Tuna sandwiches I often ate for lunch, mixed with Miracle Whip and sweet relish, and if I didn't toast the bread, I placed potato chips between the bread for a salty crunch with each bite. Because tuna came in a can (pouches didn't exist in the Eighties), I could ignore its animal origins. Fish fillets required more obvious ignorance on my part, especially as I picked through it to avoid the microscopic bones. I have no recollection of ever making the connection between fish in tanks and the fish on my plate. Usually only a summer supper in my early days as a result of Dad's fishing, fish was one of my favorite meals.

Until the day I looked in a bucket to see the fish my dad, grandpa, and uncles caught.

Sister, my cousin, and I bounded out from Grandma's house to the garage to see the buckets of fish the men brought back from Holiday Lake. As the youngest at six or seven, I followed wherever Sister and my cousin went. Sister ran to the back of the garage where uncles gutted fish. I didn't realize such disembowelment occurred in the garage. Shocked, I remained at the entrance. Not only did dead animals traumatize me, but blood and needles caused me to faint. I looked down to avoid seeing anything upsetting, which led my eyes directly into one of the many buckets sitting on the driveway.

In a large blue bucket, a half dozen fish stared back at me, their huge puppy dog eyes pleading with me to put them back in water. Their mouths puckered into an *O*, as if the chorus line of fish sang in unison. My oblivion shattered. These fish were our supper.

I didn't dare peer into the other buckets. As my sister and cousin ran off to play badminton, I panicked as to how to survive our impending meal. Sister and I were Good Little Eaters, as if we wore invisible crowns on our heads at the supper table. Good Little Eaters didn't complain about the food on their plates, ate everything without a mess, and cleaned up after themselves. My grandparents praised us on our Good Little Eater status, bragging about our good table manners and healthy appetites. I didn't want to risk losing my invisible crown over a fish.

The fish fry began with grandma, Mom, and my aunts flittering about the kitchen. My grandma dipped a gleaming white heap of what was once a fish into flour, then set it in a hot skillet, sputtering and sparkling bits of grease into the air. A familiar panic seized my chest, like when I saw a spider or had to go to the doctor. Which fish fillets came from the blue bucket?

At first my pleas were ignored. Finally, Grandma asked in her gravelly voice, "Why does it matter? They're all the same."

I blurted, "Because I don't want to eat the ones from the blue bucket."

Mom intervened, "Go sit down." I could tell by her exasperated tone that I was causing unnecessary trouble when they—the adults—already had enough to do.

Grandma said to Mom, "Why does she care what bucket they came from?"

Mom spoke in a hushed voice, so I couldn't hear her response. But I heard Grandma reply for Grandma had a voice that could carry into the next county. "Well where does she think fish come from?"

As the women plated the fish and set it on the table, I asked again, "These aren't from the blue bucket, are they?"

Mom shook her head. "No, just eat." Her tone implied I was dangerously close to losing my invisible Good Little Eater crown.

Grandpa had taken his spot at the head of the table. "Why does she care about what bucket they came from?"

When I wanted people to listen to me, no one did. I felt invisible most of the time. Now I was having an existential crisis for a child and everyone was ready to criticize.

Grandma said, "She saw those fish alive and now she doesn't want to eat them."

Grandpa scoffed. "It's a goddamn fish. What else are you going to do with it?"

I picked at the fish Mom set on my plate since I refused to serve myself. I wanted reassurance that I was not about to eat a friend, but I knew no one cared about the fish or my feelings about the fish. The filet shape allowed me to imagine a head on one end, a tail on the other, a whole fish that had just hours ago been swimming happily in a lake, saying hi to his friends. Now it was dead on my plate. I took tiny bites, thinking that would resolve whatever cannibalism I felt. Normally I took seconds. This time, I walked away from the table hungry and guilty. My oblivion had been obliterated.

I still gobbled up fish sticks, dipping them in tartar sauce, for they looked manmade and born from a factory. I ate fish fillets when forced to but pretended that the bones worried me as I picked at it, eating as little as possible.

Which exasperated my mother.

In ninth grade, I said goodbye to the large fish tank when Mom finally sold it at our garage sale. I tried to convince her that we should use it again, thinking it would be neat to have a fish tank I could remember, but she said keeping the tank clean created more work than it was worth.

That Christmas, Mom bought me a globe-shaped fish tank that could sit on my dresser in my room. I loved it—at first.

Mom took me fish shopping over Christmas break. I wanted seven tiny fish so I could name them after the characters on *thirtysomething*. The previous summer I had become obsessed with reruns of *thirtysomething* on Lifetime. Hooked after the first episode, I couldn't wait until I was thirtysomething so I could live my own life and make my own decisions. (Being thirtysomething wasn't as fun as watching the show about thirtysomethings.)

My friends couldn't understand why I liked such an old people show.

My Hope and Michael zebra fish needed to match, since they were married, and my Nancy and Elliot goldfish matched, even though they were almost divorced. My Melissa fish was bright orange to match her orangey hair while Ellyn was a black fish to match her jet-black hair. My Gary catfish had long whiskers since he had a beard and shaggy hair.

At night, my fishtank cast a subtle glow, a nightlight for teenagers. In just a couple of weeks, the light no longer filtered through the algae, which had muddied my *thirtysomething* home. Mom and I bought a little snail that was supposed to naturally clean the tank, but he couldn't keep up with the work. I stressed out my fish every time I cleaned their home, which became a two-hour long hassle every week. No wonder we abandoned the fish tank years ago.

And then Elliot died. Thank god it wasn't one of the other fish. (I'd explain but would rather have you binge-watch all four seasons to find out for yourself although no streaming service carries *thirtysomething*.)

At first, we replaced the fish as they died. The original Hope outlived all the others. It seemed more humane at the time to flush them rather than bury them. With every flush, it became easier to deal with each subsequent death. I knew my fish as well as one could know any fish, although I associated their personalities with their *thirtysomething* counterparts. I wasn't surprised when Nancy and Elliot fought or Melissa snubbed Gary or Gary ignored Melissa or even at Hope and Michael's passive aggressiveness to each other. (We later transferred the remaining fish into our smaller rectangular fish tank, which still housed at least Hope and Ellyn based on the picture I found of my room before I moved to college. Memory is a funny thing. I had no idea I had fish in my room for almost three years.)

I would forever personify every animal around me, stuffed or real, even as I aged. I accepted that every living thing would die—sort of. I just never wanted to correlate their deaths with the food on my plate.

I preferred eating tuna, fish sticks, and fish sandwiches because they looked nothing like real fish (although I secretly enjoy eating walleye at restaurants that have tartar sauce that tastes like Kraft's. Don't tell my fish friends.)

GOODBYE, MIKEY

Early summer, 1983. Lunch time.
I stood at the sink, washing what was left of the lunch dishes. I watched Sister through the window as she collected dry shirts from the clothesline, longing to do that instead of having my hands in dirty dishwater, my least favorite chore, but I was way too short to reach the clothespins clamped at the top of the clothesline.

Mom had run out after Mikey just minutes before. This happened often, especially when dogs in the neighborhood were in heat. Mikey's long legs allowed him to jump over our chain-link fence. Mom grabbed the leash from the hook in the garage and left Sister and me to finish our lunch.

As I put the dishes away—at least the ones I could reach in the lower cupboards—I heard growling from the garage. It sounded like multiple dogs, a low guttural snarl followed by an ominous bark that I had never heard before. When I opened the back door that led to the garage, I found Mom wrestling with a growling Mikey on his back, his huge, clawed paws flapping around, froth spitting from his toothy mouth. My teeny tiny mother had somehow pinned a large ferocious dog to his back. Mom and Mikey struggled right next to the steps, up against the wall that the garage shared with the house. Before my childhood mind could unravel what I was seeing, Mom yelled at me in controlled tone. "Shut the door and stay in the house."

I did as told, scared yet confused. The open back door from the garage led right to where Sister stood. I wrung my hands and paced the kitchen, wanting to open the door to see if Mom was okay. The growling stopped, leading to an eerie silence. I fought tears as I stared at the back door.

Mom and Sister entered the house together, but I can't recall through which door. Tears flowed as I ran up to Mom, "What happened? Where's Mikey?"

Mom walked straight to the sink. The bloody scrape on her breastbone silenced me. I couldn't look for fear I would faint, but when I saw it after it had scabbed over, it looked to be as wide and deep as the Grand Canyon.

Mom said, not so much to me and Sister, but herself. "I knew better than to turn my back on a mad dog." Once Mom had tracked down Mikey, put him on a leash, and led him home into the garage, she pointed her finger at him and said, "Bad dog." When she turned around to hang up the leash, Mikey attacked her. I would never know how she pinned Mikey to the ground or how she calmed him enough to get away from him.

I didn't know what to be upset about at that moment, for I was upset over everything. I feared Mom was mortally wounded, I wanted to see Mikey but now feared him... suddenly our monotonous summer day had become a nightmare, one I couldn't comprehend or articulate except with tears.

The rest of the scene blurs. After Mom patted her wound dry, she called Dad at work. Did he call Animal Control or did Mom? Sister hung close to Mom, following the line of action. I was a muddled mess, not understanding the sequence of events. What was happening?

Mom said to us, "Mikey can't be around you girls anymore because he could hurt you."

I didn't know what that meant for Mikey.

A white van pulled into our driveway. Stuff happened out of my eyesight. Through the front window, I saw the van pull away, with Mikey staring back from the barred windows. He didn't look fierce at all; in fact, he looked apologetic, his ears alert as he left our driveway for the last time. I cried, understanding fully that I would never see him again.

Dad arrived home about the same time the van left. He carried his briefcase into the house and disappeared into the kitchen to talk to Mom. He never came home from work early.

I overheard tidbits of conversation. Maybe Mikey did have some wolf in him as that would explain the ferociousness. He wasn't neutered either.

I don't remember anyone explicitly stating where Mikey had gone. Maybe it was like Santa Claus—parents don't tell children Santa isn't real and allow older siblings or cousins or friends to annihilate such dreams. I don't remember asking anyone for clarification either. In my version of the ending, Mikey frolicked in some meadow in a jail-like place where naughty dogs were sent for attacking people. Years later I would realize that Mikey was executed for his crime.

We never spoke of it. Mom didn't like to lament over life's issues. You could grieve, but you must move on. No wallowing allowed.

While I'm thankful everyone allowed me to believe that Mikey was running around playing with other thug dogs in an incarcerated setting, that would only certify my belief that animals possessed some sort of immortality that humans didn't. That puppies and kitties, even squirrels, rabbits, and deer who weren't hit by cars or shot by men in the forest, lived in immortality like some Emily Dickinson poem.

Yet perhaps that was the best decision my parents made. I didn't develop a fear of dogs, even big dogs although I preferred little ones, after witnessing Mom wrestling Mikey on the ground or seeing the gash that crusted over on her chest, most of which was visible if Mom wore a V-neck shirt.

I was most upset that I didn't get to say goodbye.

SHARING IS CARING

Care Bears came out in 1983 when I was six years old. I coveted one, even dreaming about them while I slept.

Pretty colored bears with hearts on their butts who each had a unique fairy-tale design embroidered on their tummies sounded like something I invented. That's all I talked about, hoping Santa would deliver a Care Bear down the chimney.

While I would have loved Care Bears no matter what, the timing of my Care Bears addiction coincided with Mikey's departure. I craved animals, fancying the porcelain Dalmatian on *Wheel of Fortune* or wondering why anyone would choose a car over a donkey or a goose on *Let's Make a Deal*. I desperately wanted a pet but knew I had no control over such a decision. A Care Bear was more attainable.

Except Care Bears were atrociously expensive.

In 1983, paying thirty dollars for a stuffed bear would be the equivalent of ninety dollars today (taking into account inflation). Although Dac's salary thrust us into middle class, Mom remained thrifty, clipping coupons, sewing clothes and quilts and curtains, and saving more than spending. A thirty-dollar bear was not in the budget.

Mom schemed with my aunt, who had drawn my name in our yearly Christmas gift exchange (technically the gift's tag came from my cousin). Because I was such a girlie-girl, I guess my aunt and cousin thought choosing the most boyish bear fit me best. No matter. Grumpy Bear became my darling.

Care Bears became the best object in my childhood life, tied with Barbie and MTV.

Grumpy Bear and I were travel mates, my favorite, although I never admitted it nor consciously thought it. We spent every day together. He loved playing Yahtzee, driving Barbie's pink Corvette (each leg went into a separate seat and he sat centered in the car, much like Gizmo in *Gremlins*), and swinging on the swing set. He longed for bike rides, but my pink bike did not have a basket despite how much I begged for a bike with a basket.

I had Care Bears folders, book covers, lunchboxes, Play-Doh molds, a belt, a bathroom cup, a bookbag, records, books, Valentines, stickers, shirts, pajamas, calendars, board games, a necklace and ring and pin set, and Pizza Hut drinking glasses. And even underwear. I colored bears in my Care Bears coloring books, we created Care Bears suncatchers, and baked Care Bears Shrinky Dinks. My grandparents gave me more Care Bears—by the time I was in junior high, I had eight original bears, plus Share Bear.

Cabbage Patch dolls appearing on my Christmas list would have been just as bizarre as asking for socks and tennis shoes. Sister found her coveted preemie under the tree while I still asked for Barbies and Care Bears. I didn't need baby dolls, for I treated my Care Bears like babies.

When I played house, I dressed up my Care Bears in old clothes that Grandma J had given me. I don't know if these were actual baby clothes or vintage doll clothes, but I shoved my Care Bears' fat arms into little collared Jackie Kennedy jackets, crammed their stubby legs into crochet booties, and adorned their overstuffed heads with ruffled bonnets. My Grandpa C had two different metal strollers I could push around while I clomped in my plastic high heels. That was my idea of motherhood.

I took my Care Bears everywhere, but since I only had one set of hands, I always chose Grumpy to come with me. He read with me, colored, judged Barbie pageants, and played board games. (Just recently I found name tags in our *The Price is Right* board game, with all the Care Bears' names written in Sister's artsy lettering.) Grumpy also joined me for breakfast and lunch.

On one kitchen adventure, I smeared chocolate syrup on Grumpy's belly when I made chocolate milk (Mom never bought chocolate milk—we had to make our own using Hershey's Chocolate Syrup and milk, and these were the days of the little chocolate can, not the squeeze bottle). Usually I was careful around my toys, but Grumpy insisted on helping me mix my chocolate milk, sitting on the counter just inches from my glass. When I set the spoon down, the unmixed chocolate that stuck to its end grazed Grumpy's tummy, leaving a thick brown smear across his rain cloud.

Mom took one look at Grumpy and declared he needed a bath.

By then, Grumpy had lost his bright shiny blue fur. In just over six months, he looked like a bear found inside the wall of an abandoned house in 1943. Mom couldn't wait to throw him in the washing machine.

Care Bears' washing instructions: *MACHINE WASH-ABLE. Tie toy in pillowcase, wash warm, tumble dry, medium heat. Brush plush to fluff.* Mom had waited for this day ever since Grumpy's arrival. Most stuffed animals' washing instructions were *Surface Wash Only* while Care Bears could ride the Raging Washing Machine. I panicked because Grumpy and I had many traits in common: we kept to ourselves, we hated roller coasters, and we couldn't swim. Grumpy was going underwater and being tossed about for the length of the gentle cycle.

Mom had to pull me away from the washer, assuring me, "He'll be fine."

After the washer completed its cycle, Mom opened the pillowcase so I could peek inside to verify Grumpy survived (he did, although his hair never curled again, another thing we had in common), but now the dryer tossed him around for an hour. His hefty butt remained damp, so Mom clamped his ears on the clothesline hanging across our utility room. I swear he glared at me.

Because the washing machine had straightened his hair, Grumpy visited Sister's salon. Sister, with her slim curling iron, curled Grumpy's lock of blue hair, but it only managed a slight wave at the end that wouldn't hold (she even sprayed a bit of hairspray to keep the curl). All that salon work gave Grumpy flat hair and split ends (another thing we had in common). Never again did Grumpy end up in the washer, even after a peanut butter and jelly incident. I scrubbed his arm clean as best I could without asking Mom for help.

Grumpy Bear grounded me, both literally and figuratively, in high school. By then, most of my stuffed animals stayed hidden in my closet, taking Barbie's old spot since her stuff was now stored in the cubby under the stairs. But Grumpy Bear stayed in my room, prominently displayed on my bookshelf above my CD player. While I had stopped openly speaking to my stuffed animals, telepathy always happened in those dire moments, which occurred with increasing frequency as a teenager.

Grumpy's crochety presence kept me from running off with a boy. Not that I would have *actually* run away from home, but it was fun to daydream about all the possibilities of the world outside my bedroom. But Grumpy's visage did not approve of even fantasizing about such a preposterous thought. *I'm not going anywhere. You'll have to leave me behind. And then what? What kind of a life do you think you're going to have with that loser? In two more years, we can leave together for college.* I knew Grumpy was right, but years of being Little Miss Perfect had gotten me nowhere. I had no say in my pathetic existence, so I thought anywhere was better than home. *Nonsense. No one on thirtysomething ran away from home. You'll never have such a life if you throw it all away now.* I hated when Grumpy Bear was right.

I never thought my subconscious, my inner voice, my gut would take the shape of a stuffed blue bear with a perpetual old lady puckered mouth and the personality of Thelma Harper.

Care Bears followed me into adulthood. I collected more Bears and Cousins when the twentieth anniversary ones looked like the original (I wasn't fond of all the newer styles with their flatter bodies and oddly shaped heads). When I was pregnant, I insisted on a Care Bear nursery, lining the walls with shelves of bears, creating rows of hearted paws. Mom fashioned little swings out of fabric and yarn for the smaller bears to dangle from underneath the shelves. Once I found out we were having a boy, blue became the preferred color, giving Grumpy Bear the center of attention once again. (I always wore heels and having a baby didn't change that—motherhood *was* about Care Bears and clomping around in high heels while pushing a stroller after all.) Care Bears adorned Baby JJ's first cup, plate, and spoon too. I was bummed when I couldn't find any Care Bears baby clothes, thinking how charming JJ would have looked in a little blue Grumpy Bear shirt.

Grumpy Bear came to college with me, sat on various bookshelves after I married, moving from place to place until he was needed in the nursery. He eventually earned a permanent spot in my curio cabinet, not far from Little Animal. I smile at his grumpy face every day.

HELLO AND GOODBYE, DUCHESS

I was an observant yet oblivious child. And adult. I stay in my own little world yet remain keen to my surroundings. Many times in my life I've felt left out of key information, significant information that impacts my day-to-day existence. This paradox has jolted me with a reality that I didn't see coming or maybe I just didn't want to see it.

Duchess is the perfect example.

After Mikey's departure, we never spoke about him. Once school started again, Sister and I asked for another dog. I was more Team Cat though, thinking this was the perfect time to finally get that kitty I had always dreamed about. No one heard me no matter how much I begged for a kitty. Our house remained petless.

Months later, we visited the animal shelter. I was more interested in the cats than the dogs, but we bypassed the room of cats and headed for the cemented kennel area that housed all the unclaimed dogs. I hated that experience, seeing shaking little doggie legs skitter about on cement floors while big dogs jumped at the gates. All their eyes looked sad and defeated, with little hope for a forever family. It was so much worse than garage sale stuffed animals—real live homeless dogs who longed for a forever home. It traumatized me to the point I never wanted to go back (and I still close my eyes during those Sarah McLachlan commercials).

Then after Christmas, suddenly we had a little beagle named Duchess.

Duchess was past her puppy phase. She didn't seem all that bright or responsive to what we said. We played with her outside in the snow; the only picture that exists of Duchess is in our snow fort with me and Sister on a snow day from school. Duchess was in heat; I worried about the red spots she left in the snow.

My favorite thing about Duchess was her size. She was small compared to Mikey, whose long legs had towered over me when I sat on the floor. Duchess was compact, who could sit on my lap and not overwhelm me. But she wasn't fun to pet. Her hair was short and coarse, not soft like Mikey's. I liked having someone to feed from the table again.

And then I came home from school one day and Duchess was gone.

I burst into tears.

I don't recall Mom sitting us down and telling us that we were fostering a dog. I wouldn't have much understood the word *foster* anyway. I don't recall anyone explicitly saying that this was not our forever pet. Maybe Mom did and I just didn't listen. Maybe she did and I didn't agree with the arrangement so I just blocked it out of my life. I vaguely remember Mom saying we were trying out our arrangement with Duchess, whatever that meant.

But I do remember how upset I was that no one told me the morning I left for school that Duchess would be gone by the time I returned.

Parents make decisions for all sorts of reasons. As a parent myself, I'm sure I've fucked up my son's life even when I thought I was doing the right thing. We assume kids can't handle news so we don't tell them. Maybe they won't even notice. Maybe they won't understand. And how do you know if a child truly understands what you're saying? You think they get it, only to realize they were only half paying attention when you told them. Just another reason not to tell them.

And then sometimes we don't want the hassle—the emotional toll it takes on both parent and child. We don't want the fuss. My childhood household was as fuss-free as they came.

Mom responded to my tears kindly but a bit defensively. "None of us really bonded with Duchess anyway. You girls didn't play with her all that much. She was adopted by a family who wanted her."

Considering I have little memory of interacting with Duchess, Mom must have been right, although my lack of memory could be age-related or that Duchess only lived with us for a few weeks.

Happy that Duchess had a forever home, I stopped crying. But I remained pissed that no one told me.

I didn't get to say goodbye to Mikey. And now I didn't get to say goodbye to Duchess either.

COWS ARE PEOPLE, TOO

I am guilty of caterpillar torture and murder. Or at least for my complacency during the crime.

Sister, my cousin, and I found a caterpillar in the park near my grandma's house, probably when I was in second or third grade. This caterpillar looked like something from a horror movie: yellow mohawk threads protruded from its gargantuan thick green body. After my initial disgust, it fascinated me as its body moved like a wave. Its little filament feet appeared to grip the sidewalk. Either Sister or my cousin picked up a stick for the caterpillar to climb on then placed the stick at the end of the tornado slide. We discussed what would happen if we stepped on it: green slime or blood? My cousin took the stick and stabbed the caterpillar. More like yellow slime. We watched it writhe for a while, oozing sticky slime. My cousin and my sister stabbed it a couple more times. Did they flick it into the sand, or did they eventually step on it? I walked away from the park, heavy, but not sure why. We killed bugs all the time—I didn't exactly, usually calling for help to have someone else do it. Spiders deserved to die and crickets creeped me out with their crunchy bodies and wasps and bees had stingers to fear. I stepped on countless ants without thinking. But that caterpillar—wouldn't it have turned into a butterfly? And if we were going to kill it anyway, why didn't we just step on it rather than torture it?

I thought of that caterpillar every time we went to that park.

I thought animals (and caterpillars apparently) lived like people, just not with a language that used words or a world that centered around consumerism (they didn't have any pockets to keep their money, except kangaroos). I put myself in their place, wondering what they thought about life with humans.

I hated Civil War paintings and movies. War confused me from an early age anyway, especially those wars before tanks and machine guns. I didn't understand how rational human beings—men only—could run straight to the enemy, with machetes or bayonets or medieval torture devices and then hack away at whoever steps near them. Wouldn't you injure or kill people from your own side? I couldn't fathom such a thing as a five-year-old and I still can't at 45. (Is war a necessary evil?) Add in some horses and I cringed even more for the horses didn't choose to go to battle (the Vietnam War would later teach me that not everyone in uniform wanted to fight), the fruitlessness of it all, and the idiocracy of solving conflicts with violence. I wondered what the horses thought.

"These men are so stupid. Hey, Bob, how's your neck?"

"It hurts, man. That idiot jerked the reins when he got

shot. He deserved it with his horrible aim. I'm lucky to be standing here."

More horses join in. "We're thinking of making a run for it to that apple orchard we passed a few miles back. The lower apples have all been pillaged, but we can reach the higher ones."

"Yeah, hopefully no one will find us there. These men are morons."

I had a love-hate relationship with zoos.

Tigers paced around on concrete floors in cages that barely allowed them to take five steps (this was before zoos constructed natural habitats for their inhabitants). I felt their unhappiness as they had nothing to do all day but walk back and forth in their jail cell. The areas that had grass and rocks and trees I thought the animals might enjoy. If I were a zebra, I would prefer living inside a secure place without the threat of a lion attack. You'd never have to worry about food and even have shelter in bad weather. But would they understand our Midwestern weather?

"Stripe, what the fuck is this cold white shit falling from the sky?"

"How the hell would I know?"

"Hey, you. Yeah, you, Ostrich. You've been here awhile. What the hell is this white wet shit and why am I shivering?"

Ostrich wanders over. "Get used to it. They call it snow and it's abominable. Wait until the wind picks up. The cold season here is longer than the warm season. Doesn't seem to keep those fool humans away either. By the way, the name's Alexander."

I longed to rescue skittish foxes and bring them home with me. Imagine living locked in a fenced area with people coming by every single day for the rest of your life (minus Thanksgiving, Christmas, and Easter). No place to hide, no peace and quiet, just a constant stream of looky-loos and screaming babies.

Yet I longed to be one of those looky-loos. Despite my insistence, we never went to the zoo—which was less than five miles from our house. I only visited the zoo during school field trips. I could hardly contain my excitement on those rare days, yet the forced group marches each class had to maintain during our trip defeated the fun. We stood around the monkeys, my least favorite, forever, but only saw the brown bears for two seconds.

Once I started driving, the zoo was the first place I drove to on my own (other than to my job as a grocery store bagger). My peers probably snuck out to a party that served beer, while I planned what felt like a wildlife adventure. I convinced two friends to accompany me; neither matched my enthusiasm. My best friend threatened to smack me if I said, "Oh, he's so cute," one more time.

I bought a zoo membership when my son was four—we'd walk around the zoo three to four times a month. He loved to amble about the sidewalks and bridges and always wanted to ride the train, which took us behind the African Safari. He declared at just five years old, "I'm too old to ride the carousel." Now that he's in college, he will still accompany me on my yearly zoo trip to see the red panda.

The circus—another animal activity I fantasized about as a child (that and having a pony at all birthday parties). I begged Mom every year to go to the circus. All elementary school children received free tickets for the Shriner's Circus, but every year Mom told me no. With the help of my Grandpa C, I finally attended the circus. I thought I would see dogs in hats riding bikes and bears dressed as clowns and pretty horses in tasseled hats prancing in a circle. The only animals I saw were dogs that jumped through hoops. It wasn't as animal centric as I had anticipated.

In college, I went to the circus with my best friend. We bought plastic junk since the one time I went as a child I missed out on such crap. Three rings going at once over-stimulated my senses and I didn't know what to watch. I don't remember that as a problem the one time I went as a child, although my ten-year-old self was probably overstimulated just by leaving the house at night.

As a parent, when I took three-year-old JJ to the circus, he rode the elephant. His small hands clapped at everything, sometimes with a little "oooh" escaping his lips.

Road trips—seldom as they were—gave me much to ponder in the animal world. Roadkill I'd rather not acknowledge. I looked away (still do), hoping the driver did everything possible to avoid hitting the poor creature. I have thus far never killed an animal with a car, except a suicidal bird, who flew into the grill of my convertible while I drove 80 mph on the interstate. I felt horrible but rationalized that I couldn't stop a bird's death wish. If I ever hit a squirrel or a bunny or a deer, I probably will never drive again.

I wondered if deer noticed a missing member and if they knew it was dead on the highway. (Same with squirrels and bunnies and raccoons.) Do they do a count every evening and every morning, checking attendance? If so, do they send out a search party or just assume the worst? Do they think *glad it wasn't me* and continue with their day? Do they go back and tell everyone else what happened? "Guys, Joey didn't make it across." Dolphins, geese, elephants, and even squirrels mourn the death of their mate and/or babies. What happens to all the widowed and orphaned animals in the wild?

In the Midwest, cows are abundant landmarks seen from the interstate. Despite their upright, still lifestyle, their behavior fascinates me. The one standing in the middle of the creek—was he being bullied and ridiculed like a criminal in a pillory or was he the popular one that all other cows envied?

"Yeah, you go, Bertha!"

One cow might whisper to another cow, "Can't someone else stand in the water for once?" Followed by an eye roll.

When I see a lone cow standing off by himself, I worry he's depressed or left out of the group. Or lost. Or separated from his best friend (cows do have besties and they show signs of depression when separated).

Lost pet posters hang on my brain for hours. How can owners live without their beloved pet? And what did the dog or cat think? Were they sad and lonely and panicked, unable to find their way home? Were they a victim of a dog-nap or cat-nap? Or did they celebrate their change in scenery?

Seeing a mother duckling and her babies walking around the neighborhood sends me into rescue mode. The nearest pond is, well, not anywhere nearby. Where are they going? I'd like to put them all in my car and drive them safely to their destination.

I know I need to trust that nature knows what it's doing. It's humans that cause the chaos, but I don't like that nature isn't sentimental or nostalgic. It just is. Like the little turtles that end up on their backs and can't flip themselves over. Why don't cameramen flip over the turtles? Why don't they intervene when they see a lion stalking a herd of zebras? Blow a horn, shoo them away. I understand natural selection, but I don't *understand* it.

My stuffed animals possessed people personalities and people problems, so live ones must too. But I could rescue my stuffed animals, unlike the real ones in nature. Mom even contributed to my need to save them (the stuffed ones, at least).

Christmas morning when I was eight, a stuffed brown he's-so-ugly-he's-cute wrinkle dog sat under the tree with a note tied around his neck. The envelope had my name on it. I looked at Mom, confused. She said, "You better open it."

I removed the sparkly green ribbon from around the soft dog's neck. Inside the envelope was a card with a sleigh on the front. I read the handwritten note aloud. "*Dear Julie, I need a favor from you. I need you to take care of this puppy for me. You see, his Mom and Dad were helping me with my holiday planning in Russia (that's where he comes from) when they were caught in a snowstorm and they perished. He's an orphan and I knew how much you loved all of your animals. I am hoping you will have a little more room in your heart to give Twinkie (that's his name) the love he needs right now.*

Thanks, Santa."

It almost brought tears to my eyes. "He doesn't have any parents?" I grabbed him and hugged him close to me. Mom smiled. I said, "He'll never be lonely with all my other animals to play with." I kept him on my lap as I opened the rest of my presents. He suffered through a day of Barbies and even ate with me at the supper table.

I found out about Santa shortly after that Christmas, so Mom told me the story behind Twinkie. "I fell in love with the ugly thing, but I didn't know if you would like him or not. I wrote the letter to explain why I bought such an ugly dog."

"Did you have to kill off his parents?"

"I knew you wouldn't be able to resist him that way."

"And Russia?"

She smirked. "I wanted to give him a unique history."

That's what I seem to do with every animal encounter. In those passing seconds on the highway, I've created a life for those cows, hoping they're happy, with cartoonish problems that will save them from their fate.

It's the animal world that has the power to restore my faith in humanity. When a gaggle of geese lollygag across a busy street with a 40-mph speed limit, both sides of traffic stop. We wait patiently as those feathered babies walk across, unaware of the traffic jam they might be causing. No one honks their horn. No one shouts. We wait as the line of ducklings pass in front of us, accepting such an interruption in our overstimulated, hectic days. I return to such moments when I watch the news and everyone hates everyone else. I want to scream at the television, "But we all worked together and let those babies cross the road! Why can't we compromise now?"

HELLO, ELSA

My family rarely suffered from spontaneity, impulsivity a travesty. After Duchess, Mom spent over a year planning for our perfect dog.

In those days, newspaper ads, word of mouth, or pet stores were the primary ways to find the exact breed of dog you wanted. For reasons only Mom knows, she decided on a Norwegian elkhound.

Such a decision might link to our ancestors who came from Sweden and Norway. An elkhound is a practical medium-sized dog, not a hyperactive lap dog. Mom bought a book on Norwegian elkhounds; according to the receipt I found inside it, Mom purchased the book for $5.25—on December 18. A new puppy wouldn't join us until summer.

Anticipation halts time for a child. Every night I went to sleep I dreamed about our new puppy, making Christmas morning feel like just another day. A puppy would last forever, not just one morning of present opening. When Christmas passed without a puppy under the tree, I had given up, accepting my petless life, settling for the stuffed animals who had become my best friends. Sister graduated from elementary school that spring, so I could no longer rely on her to play for she had developed Big Girl Problems with junior high looming in the fall.

Early that summer, Mom announced: "We've found our puppy!" She probably didn't say it like that, but that's how my brain interpreted the message. On that blessed summer weekend, we drove an hour to a small town in Iowa. A farmhouse with dirt roads greeted us, as well as a litter of puppies. Had we had a four-door car like every other family in America, I would have bolted from it and raced into the pile of puppies. Instead, I had to wait for Mom to exit the car, then pull the seat up so I could step out of our two-door boat-like Thunderbird. The puppies' gentle yips and patter of tiny paws on the dirt immediately soothed all my other senses, yet I remained overstimulated by all the baby activity happening just feet away.

All the puppies bore black snouts, which melded into the dirt they rolled around in. Their tiny ears seemed too small for their noticeable noses yet matched their tiny stubby legs. Itty-bitty curly tails wiggled uncontrollably from furry butts.

Sister and I were well-behaved children 99 percent of the time in public, so I followed Mom's lead even though I wanted nothing more than to squeal and pick up all the puppies I could hold and spin around in circles with them. Mom sat down outside the cluster of rolling puppies and told us, "Let them come to you."

In a previous life Mom was a queen, Cleopatra perhaps, as she commanded the animals around her. Some pups ran straight to her, then in their puppiness quickly abandoned her to roll around again with their siblings. But one pup seemed more interested in Mom than the rest. She crawled on Mom and remained there as Mom pet her. When she started to walk away, Mom gently cooed at her and held out her hand, and the puppy returned to investigate, sniffing Mom's fingers. Our puppy had chosen us.

The rest of the particulars, like the exchange of money and paperwork, only adults might remember. I remember that overwhelming happiness that you try to tame so it doesn't burst out into a theatrical spectacle of song and dance. This puppy was better than a Barbie wrapped under the Christmas tree, and that's difficult to top. I imagined my life with my forever friend: walks, running around the yard, cuddling on the couch while watching television, even a good listener while I chatted about whatever was on my nine-year-old mind. My life forever changed for the better.

Even though I didn't know the reference at the time, I had a little bit of *Of Mice and Men*'s Lennie in me. I wanted to pet and hug the soft furry baby nonstop, so I worked to contain myself and not hug the puppy to death. I held her only briefly anyway, since she had a case of the wiggles and I feared I might drop her. I liked her on my lap much more.

In preparation for our trip, Dad brought a cardboard box for our new puppy to sleep in on the ride home. Sister and I set the box on the hump between our seats that separated our legroom, but our new puppy preferred to crawl on us, eventually crawling around Sister's back and lying there until Sister couldn't lean forward anymore. I couldn't wait to get home to play with her, but Mom had to remind me again, "Puppies sleep a lot at first."

Mom gave our new puppy an authentic Norwegian

name: Elsa. Years later when Disney released that obnoxious movie *Frozen*, I giggled at the name of the protagonist. Long before Elsa made its way into popular culture and became trendy, we had a Norwegian elkhound named that in 1986.

Potty training or other puppy dos and don'ts hold no place in my memories. Mom, an expert at nursing and training baby animals (and humans), probably accomplished the tasks in record time. Elsa spent much of her day outside. Much to my disappointment, she would not be sharing a bed with me. Dad constructed a wooden bed for her and lined it with carpet scraps, which he placed in the garage. She was not allowed on furniture either (at least when Mom and Dad were around).

That summer, I spent more time outdoors than ever before. Sister and I ran through the sprinkler with her, took her for walks on the bike path behind our house, and tried to teach her to fetch. Dad didn't wrestle with her like he did with Mikey. Elsa remained calm, rarely barked, and rarely got in trouble.

Elsa quickly outgrew the ability to nap under the couch with her little head popped out, instead wedging herself up against the couch with her snout underneath it. By the time school started, I could no longer pick her up and snuggle with her, although she loved leaning up against me as we sat on the floor. I hugged her several times a day.

Mom said Elsa understood the hierarchy in the family: Mom was in charge (and Dad too), but she knew she could get away with things around me and Sister.

That's how I treated Elsa—like she was my sister, not my pet.

LOVE, ELSA

Elsa became my parents' third daughter, at least in my mind.

Elsa sat with us as we watched television at night. She had a habit of sitting more on one hip than the other, leaning against either Dad's recliner or Mom's chair, where an arm could rest or dangle and pet her. She sat patiently at the table during supper, always next to me. I shared a comradery with Elsa only siblings understood.

The basement was our own private play space. Sister and I let her climb on the couch and the fabric-covered rocking chair. We snapped pictures of her, looking happily guilty as she sat on basement furniture or on our beds at Grandpa C's house. The film roll would take forever to fill and then develop, so her secret was safe with us.

I even gave Elsa a couple of my stuffed animals. One was a floppy fabric panel dog I found at a garage sale. With no buttons or other plastic pieces, it was perfect for puppies. I had flashbacks of *The Velveteen Rabbit* when Mom threw away all Elsa's stuffed toys after one of our cousin's dogs had fleas.

Elsa knew what belonged to her, what she could chew on and slobber on and play with. We didn't find chewed up shoes or mopboards or furniture legs. Elsa never bothered my stuffed animals, as if sensing those were not hers to destroy. Other than absconding with Mom's slippers so we would chase after her and carrying buckets around the backyard, there were only two items Elsa coveted that didn't belong to her: my Barbies' shoes and my mint ChapStick.

I was one of those children who never lost anything—no toys, no school supplies, no socks (because I never wore socks), no jewelry, no barrettes. My first Barbie, Golden Dream Barbie, lost all the many pieces of her outfit as her gold lamé pantsuit unraveled with each wearing. My second Barbie, Roller Skating Barbie, I played with until her purple satin jacket fell apart and her hair fell out and the wheels on her roller skates came off never to be found again. But that was when I was only four years old. Since then, I had never lost a Barbie shoe, a Barbie accessory—only Beauty's dog crown had broken due to my constant use of it (it was a crown, after all). I didn't even lose a microscopic fork, spoon, or knife from my Barbie Dream Kitchen. So when a pair of beloved Barbie heels went missing—the magenta closed-toe ones—I tore my room apart and retraced my steps. At the time, I couldn't live without those hot pink heels that had come with a rare store-bought reversible dress (Mom made 99 percent of my Barbie clothes, but I purchased some dresses just for the shoes and accessories).

I had seen Elsa come out of my room right before I noticed the shoes missing. We concluded that Elsa ate them.

Mom offered a solution. "Look through the dog poop

tomorrow."

My neurotic need for those heels overpowered my disgust at digging through dog poop. After walking our large yard back and forth and up and down, Barbie's hot pink heels revealed themselves, stuck together in the same hardened brown turd. The garden trowel helped me dislodge them from the whole turd, but poop filled the inside of each shoe. After soaking them in a bucket of soap and hot water, I sprayed them free of poo, then rewashed them one more time. Too bad Clorox wipes weren't a thing in the Eighties (if they were, Mom never bought them). From then on, I shut my bedroom door when I played Barbies.

I didn't stay mad at Elsa for long, if at all. I never wanted to dig through dog poop again, but at least I found the shoes. I explained to Elsa that Barbie shoes were not for eating. She responded with that ear-back look, the innocent eyes that seemed to say, "It is impossible to be mad at me with this face."

The ChapStick was another matter.

To this day, I must always have either lipstick, lip gloss, or lip balm on my lips, which started almost as soon I was out of the womb. Like every other young girl, Cherry Chap-Stick was an essential part of living: shoved into pockets or added to little coin purses. Smear enough Cherry Chap-Stick on your lips and you can leave behind a faint pink smudge on glasses, straws, and candy cigarettes. After years of constant use, my lips said enough and developed a flaky, red rash that cracked at the corner of my lips, which burned and even felt hot to the touch. Mom bought me the black tube of ChapStick, the original, which smelled like old people to me. Then we discovered Mint ChapStick.

I carried my Mint ChapStick everywhere; if I didn't have pockets, I set it on end tables and counters and nightstands, always within arm's reach. It started disappearing. We'd find the skeleton of the tube, gutted of its minty paste, with the jagged circular end and attached stick on the carpet. Sometimes we'd find the lid, sometimes not.

Elsa viewed Mint ChapStick as a delicacy. We caught her in the act several times. Her ears went back, her eyes bulged, her tail wagged as she tried to wiggle herself away from us. I hated to take it away from her when she looked so cute, so innocent with the evidence grasped tightly in her clamped mouth. Elsa's mint ChapStick days ended when I started wearing Revlon's Copperglaze Brown lipstick in ninth grade.

I started signing Elsa's name on greeting cards.

On Mom's and Dad's birthday cards and Mother's Day/Father's Day cards, Sister signed her name with her artsy script. Then I would sign *Love, Julie and Elsa* in my juvenile handwriting.

I wrote about Elsa all the time at school. In an autobiographical packet we created in fifth grade, I wrote Elsa under the *People I Love* category, third behind my mom and dad. My sister did not make the list by name but was lumped into the category of *Relatives*. Under *I Am Loved*, Elsa showed her love by *licking me, wagging her tail, hugging me, and shaking hands.* I also daydreamed about Elsa and wrote under my happiest moment: *when we got Elsa.* In that 12-page booklet, I wrote about Elsa eight times.

By the time I started sixth grade, Elsa no longer slept in the garage.

My parents claimed a critter had snuck into the garage and scared Elsa because she would whine and scratch at the door shortly after Mom put her to bed. Elsa had never behaved in such a way. To avoid sleeping in the garage, Elsa hid under the pool table in the basement at bedtime. My parents gave up, letting her sleep in the house.

I don't think anything scared her in the garage. I think she found out what she was missing inside and didn't want to sleep in a cold or hot garage anymore. She was slowly morphing into a DogHuman.

By then, Sister and I added Elsa to our Christmas gift giving list. Mom said, "If that's how you want to spend your own money." Sister and I bought Elsa a blue ducky and wrapped it and set it under the tree. My parents laughed as they watched Elsa tear open her lone gift. Once she freed it from the paper, she walked around with it in her mouth, her tail wiggling as she showed off her present.

Every year after, Elsa had multiple presents under the tree. Mom couldn't resist, hanging up a stocking for Elsa, stuffing it with extra bones and treats. I preferred shopping in the toy section rather than the pet section; in the Eighties, pet departments sold more practical toys, ones that didn't look like children's stuffed toys. We found a monkey hanging on an endcap, with long legs and arms, perfect for Tug of War, with Velcro hands and feet for more playtime fun. I didn't like monkeys, so I didn't care if Elsa tore him apart. We latched the monkey's paws around her neck, and she whipped it about. Dad named it Aids Monkey (it was the Eighties, not that that excuses our political incorrectness). Aids Monkey remained her go-to toy for the rest of her life, somehow avoiding a total destuffing or delimbing.

Just like the rest of us, Elsa received birthday presents. Elsa and Mom shared the same birthday (poor Mom, never even having a day all to herself). I even sent Elsa a birthday card when I was in college. On the front was a Twinkie-looking dog. On the inside it read *happy birthday to someone who's ever so special to me!* I must have sent a gift with it because I wrote at the bottom *Hope you liked the squeaky bunny! Miss you!*

Elsa completed her transformation from a dog into a furry four-legged human-like member of our family. She hung out with us every night in front of the television, a time she enjoyed most. She preferred the water from the fridge as opposed to tap water. She knew when to stay out of Mom's way with the vacuum and knew not to root through my pile of stuffed animals. Elsa wasn't moody like my sister, ever reliable when I needed a friend. Elsa was no longer just The Dog.

As an adult, I uncovered old Christmas cards Mom had sent my grandparents. After she signed our names, she added *& Elsa* in her beautiful cursive writing.

BEST IN SHOW

Nobody seemed to know what a Norwegian elkhound looked like, so I always described Elsa as a wolf with a curly tail. Her coloring was much like a wolf, with furry blacks and grays, but her stockier build and wider girth differed greatly from the long legs and lean frame of a wolf. Yet my description always received oohs and aahs. In her younger, fit days, Elsa was an exotic looking dog.

One visit to our grandparents' houses coincided with the town's summer festival. At the caterpillar park, there were games and tables full of trinkets to buy. And in the afternoon, a pet show.

We had to enter Elsa.

The specifics elude me, only that you had to walk your dog around a circle. How I wanted to parade Elsa around and win the grand prize. But my invisibility had taken over by then.

Mom described me as outgoing in my baby book when I was a year old. With an older sister who adored attention, I felt invisible at home. Sister spoke for me when adults asked me questions. Mom would say, "Let Julie talk," but by then adults were more interested in our sisterly dynamic than anything I could say. At first, I didn't mind; Sister usually answered correctly for me. Plus, at school I became a social bug, unencumbered and independent. Before we moved across town during my kindergarten year, the teacher more or less told me to shut up, that everyone was tired of listening to me talk about our upcoming move and our new house. Stung, I never spoke again unless directed to; teachers in subsequent years described me as shy. My close friends would say the opposite—that I was the chatterbox. I hated giving presentations or even answering teacher's questions unless I knew I had the right answer. I volunteered little information. As the ideal student, it was shockingly easy to remain invisible in the classroom. School came easy for me: I never needed any help, I did what I was told, and I entertained myself quietly while I waited forever for everyone else to finish their work. I spent more time daydreaming and staring out the window during all the wait time than I did on schoolwork. On fourth grade standardized tests, I scored at the end of the eighth-grade year. Talk ensued about skipping fifth grade, conversations that never involved me. It was decided that I shouldn't skip a grade because of social concerns relating to my supposed shyness. My attitude was one of *whatever*. I learned I had little control over my world so don't bother to fight it (whatever *it* may be).

But this attitude, this I-could-be-going-into-sixth-grade-this-year-but-now-I'm-just-like-all-the-other-fifth-graders, was where I found myself panicked and conflicted at the park that day: I wanted to walk Elsa in the dog show but I didn't want to force myself into that uncomfortable spotlight of attention. What if I tripped? What if Elsa tugged on the leash (although she rarely did)? And then *why I am even thinking about this anyway? Of course, Sister is going to do it.*

As usual, Sister took charge, taking Elsa's leash, with every intent of parading Elsa around in the competition. But after seeing all the little kids—many even younger than me—bowed out. She tried to hand me the leash, and said, "You should do it." Mom, too, acted as if I should do it. I shook my head, frozen since I couldn't prepare. I couldn't plan. I couldn't come up with an alternative for every What If scenario should something happen: What if I had to introduce myself or say something about our pet? What if I had to stand there forever and Elsa got bored? What if I messed up? I don't know what I could have messed up, considering this was a small town, park pet show, with the only prop a table for the judges. People randomly stood off to the side in every direction talking amongst themselves. I acted as if this was a *Toddlers and Tiaras* competition (although this was decades before I'd know about such pageants), yet I didn't want to make a mistake. I didn't want Elsa to lose because of me, especially when I thought she could win. I told Sister to do it. Because the competition was seconds away from starting, neither Sister nor Mom had time to convince me. I wish one of them had shoved me into the line of little kids with their pets (although then I would be writing a different story, one where they were mean and made me do it).

Instead, I did what I did best: stayed in the background and sized up the competition while Sister took her place with the other contestants. Elsa stood out amongst the ordinary dogs: multiple bland-colored schnauzers and mean-looking Doberman pinschers, a Great Dane who looked nothing like Scooby-Doo, a golden retriever puppy, a pretty collie, and a chihuahua. The collie was the only dog that could compete with Elsa. Little kids held onto small cats and turtles, which stayed mostly hidden in their grasp. Elsa stood out with her gray and black fur, but it was her curly tail that set her apart from the rest.

An audible gasp rang in the air as Elsa showed off for the crowd. She didn't pull on the leash, dutifully walking beside Sister, her ears alert and her head poised. Some women behind me said, "Have you ever seen such a beautiful dog? I've never seen anything like it." I knew Elsa had won. Sister had Elsa sit and shake when they finished, which brought chuckles from the crowd, further cementing her win. (If I would have led Elsa around the circle, I wouldn't have thought to have her shake at the end.)

Elsa won—the top prize at a dog show: Best In Show.

The last words in Mom's Norwegian elkhound book prophesized this win: "It would be hard to find a more handsome dog, as you note from the number of compliments received when he appears in public with you."

Then came the best part: A picture in the newspaper. Except I wasn't allowed in the picture.

Mom argued with the snuffy lady in charge that I was also owner of Elsa. Mom was never one to cause a scene, but she fought for me that afternoon over a silly newspaper picture. Mom rolled her eyes (and referred to the woman as an old biddy once we got home). In the picture, Sister stands next to Elsa with the other category winners. Some no-name kitten won second place for smallest (who enters a kitten without a name—and who even owns a kitten without a name?). Sister looks like Kareem Abdul-Jabbar compared to the little kids standing next to her. Dead center in the background is some creepy balding guy with sunglasses—what we would consider a photobomb today—and off to the side in the back I see my cousin with her glasses reflecting in the sun. I guess the newspaper bitch thought it would look funny if two kids stood next to the winning dog.

Elsa not only won a ribbon, but a plastic mint green double dish. She picked it up and carried it around as though she knew she had won it. That was the dish she used until she died; Mom saved it and gave it to me.

I longed for a trophy, but Elsa only received a First Place purple ribbon.

Years later, Sister insisted we put Elsa into the *Who's Who of Pets* in 1996. Elsa's entry stated this: *Favorite activities include sleeping, social eating, shelling peanuts, romping in the snow, opening presents, stealing Mom's slippers, and burying pancakes, waffles, and French toast.*

The book was printed the year she died.

But that was still in the future. In her younger days, when we came back to that small Iowa town those next couple of years, people remembered Elsa, or at least seeing her picture in the paper. She was famous in those parts.

I would regret not leading Elsa around the circle, the first of many regrets stemming from my invisibility. Even when such circumstances were handed to me, like that sunny day in the park, I would shirk to the background, more comfortable in the shadows where people wouldn't have the opportunity to pick me apart, to judge me, to criticize me. I should have realized that everyone would be staring at Elsa—that she would be the center of attention, not me.

HOLIDAY TURKEYS

Before Napoleon Dynamite shoved tots into his pants pockets, I hid napkins full of turkey in my pockets. All for the dogs at Thanksgiving and Christmas.

Our routine when we went to my grandparents' houses in Iowa: My dad's parents lived in town, where we spent our late afternoons and evenings; around eight or nine o'clock at night, we drove about a mile outside of town to my mom's parents' farm, where we slept and spent our mornings, then went back into town mid-afternoon. Repeat until we left for home.

At first, Elsa followed us back and forth. She loved running around the farm, free of her fenced-in backyard. One time, Mom returned to the house breathless. "I almost lost her. She must have been on the scent of a deer." We trusted Elsa enough not to run away, but I always used a leash when I took her outside—just in case.

In town, Elsa liked the excitement, chaos, and people, which didn't happen at home. She enjoyed spending time with her cousins, Clyde and Summer Sausage. At least I think she did.

Elsa was the largest; Clyde was a lollygagging basset hound and Summer Sausage was a high-strung beagle. If they were Winnie-the-Pooh characters, Elsa was Pooh, Clyde was Eeyore, and Summer Sausage was Tigger. They appeared to get along although both Elsa and Clyde had little patience for the newest member of their group—Summer Sausage.

In town, Elsa, Clyde, and Summer Sausage were banished to the three-season front porch covered in Brady Bunch grass, which was unbearably cold in the winter and stifling hot in the summer. The three dogs stared at us through the family room window, all sitting quietly with their big sad eyes pleading to come inside.

The poor dogs were baffled by such neglect since in their own homes they were spoiled puppies. At my grandma's house, no adult openly babied their dogs. When all us cousins swapped stories, the tough exteriors our parents displayed toward the dogs were inaccurate representations.

While Elsa loved opening her Christmas presents at home (I begged Mom for Elsa and Clyde to exchange names for Christmas, but that resulted in a firm *no*), turkey was her favorite part of the holidays. She waited patiently when Mom took the turkey out of the oven and let it rest on the counter, then sat underfoot for her favorite moment: the carving of the turkey because Dad gave her the skin. I fed her plenty from the table and she licked all the gravy from our plates. Once the gluttony ended, she plopped on her side, bloated and napping after dinner, just like the rest of us. She equally loved turkey leftovers but missed out on Dad's late night turkey sandwich when she slept out in the garage. Dad put her to bed early so he could enjoy his sandwich without a dog watching his every bite.

But Elsa would not be celebrating with extended family.

Before the holiday festivities started, Sister, my cousin, and I would don our winter coats and sit on the porch keeping our poor pooches company. They could smell the turkey cooking, but they would not be dining with us. That didn't mean they'd go without turkey.

Grandma skimped on food during the holidays. Her motto: one potato a person. She bought a twenty-pound turkey to feed more than fifteen people. (For just the four of us at home, Mom bought at least a twenty pounder, if not bigger.) Imagine the scene from *Mickey's Christmas Carol*, when Scrooge is peering into Cratchit's home after Tiny Tim hobbles down the steps, and Bob gives Tiny Tim the whole leg, then slices the rest into barely-there pieces to feed the remaining four people. That was what Grandma J's holiday meal felt like for us girls, who, no matter how old we got, were stuck at the far end of the table—the dreaded Kiddie Table.

By the time the turkey platter arrived at the Kiddie Table, only tidbits remained. Shreds of turkey littered the platter. Sometimes we'd divvy up one large spoonful of potatoes between us. Ironically, the gravy never ran out. (And no one ate any peas and carrots.)

I used my invisibility to solve the dog starvation problem. (Okay, they weren't starving, only deprived of their holiday turkey.)

Sister, as the oldest, thrived in the spotlight. My cousin was one year older than me and just as extroverted as Sister. As the third wheel, I felt barely visible as they competed to outdo each other.

The dogs were grateful for my invisibility.

I put as much turkey on my plate that wouldn't draw suspicion, which depended on how many scraps remained once the platter found its way to the Kiddie Table. After spooning my rationed share of mashed potatoes on my plate, I put a dollop of peas and carrots next to them (but not touching). I piled my pathetic ration of potatoes as high as I could, like *Close Encounters of the Third Kind*, and carefully poured gravy into the mashed potato pond for the gravy couldn't soak the turkey or else it would be too messy to transport. I positioned my plate so the mound of potatoes blocked the view of my turkey. The Kiddie Table was always at the end of the adult table and sat near the kitchen, so any insies-outsies of aunts performing refills of gravy, rolls, or whatnot would send them right by our table. However, all the women looked mildly irritated and/or frustrated with the prep and proceedings anyway as to not pay attention to what I may or may not be doing with the food on my plate, thanks to my Good Little Eater status and my invisibility.

An open napkin lined my palm, which I rested in my lap. Intermittently throughout the meal, I'd graze my eating hand across my plate to grab a piece of turkey, close my fist, put my hand in my lap, then transfer the turkey into the napkin. Once the napkin was full, I'd stuff it in my pocket, not unlike Napoleon Dynamite with his tots, except my pants' pockets didn't have zippers. One bigger turkey year, I filled two napkins. I didn't enjoy much of my meal. If anyone caught me, particularly my Grandpa, I feared public humiliation and banishment (and the loss of my invisible Good Little Eater crown). I filled my belly with mashed potatoes and Jell-O salad (I'd eat plenty of candy later anyway).

Since the adults sat around and talked and smoked after they finished eating, we girls disappeared from the table for a while before our dishwashing began. While Sister and my cousin ventured upstairs, I dawdled, then snuck out onto the porch. All three dogs crowded around me, dying for human contact (or more likely the turkey in my pocket). I thanked them for being well-behaved, since they could have easily knocked me over (until I hit puberty which gave me breeder hips). I choreographed the distribution of turkey so all had a piece at the same time (giving Elsa the bigger pieces). When I ran out, their sad eyes and distinct frowns made me wish I had taken more. After sniffing my hands to double check, they'd bend their heads in defeat. Their only hope now was freedom—maybe I would leave the door open. Once the door closed, that too caused more head hangings and even some audible sighs of mawkish disbelief.

If only Clyde and Elsa came for Christmas, the moms would scrape off the plates and give each dog one plate of scraps (one dog would eat in the kitchen while the other remained on the porch as to avoid fighting). But I couldn't sneak extras onto the plates.

Once the dogs were deemed an unnecessary hassle, everyone left their dogs at home. Elsa's sad face loomed by the door as we left Grandpa C's, but I would still sneak a napkin of turkey and stuff it in my coat pocket. When we went back to Grandpa C's for the night, I gave it to Elsa when no one was around.

I never minded sacrificing my turkey to make Elsa happy, for she adored turkey much more than I did. This

would become the norm for me—feeding dogs food I was
supposed to eat.

DOG FIGHT

I never saw my parents fight, at least not a real fight. They argued over piddly things, like the year of a song or who starred in a movie, with the winner yelling out an "I told you so" months later (once the internet became a thing, it solved such debates immediately). They didn't always agree, but they never fought in front of us, nor did we ever hear them raise their voices to each other behind closed doors. The most discontent I witnessed between them regarded trips to my grandparents' houses. Mom hated to travel, especially in the winter. The six-hour drive (in the days when the speed limit was just 55 mph) caused Mom to worry about the weather and road conditions. Dad didn't understand her anxiety since she wasn't the one driving. Mom's pursed lips revealed her stress—she didn't bother to hide her lackluster attitude toward the trip.

Otherwise, all parental stress, including financial, extended family, even the inner turmoil of Dad's work, I knew little about. Even though I was much more observant than Sister, keen on reading people's facial expressions and overanalyzing tone of voice, I had few worries in elementary school that anything was amiss at home. If we woke to find Dad sleeping on the couch, it was due to insomnia. Iowa football games prompted the most yelling and swearing, a hostile cloud over the house even if they managed to win because according to Dad, "They played like shit." Until Sister hit puberty (or puberty hit Sister, it's hard to say), our household operated in relative monotony: calm, with no chaos allowed.

But in fifth grade, I was convinced my parents were going to get a divorce. The reason: Elsa.

One early spring weekend, Sister and I sensed an unusual tension. We escaped to the basement but could still hear my parents talking upstairs. Talking wasn't quite the word for it. Mom's pissed off tone contained more than just irritation—frustration, exasperation, fed up as she spit words at Dad. Sister and I couldn't hear all of it, but we heard Mom clearly say, "You show more affection to that damn dog than you do to me."

I couldn't breathe. Not only were my parents fighting, like a real fight, not just annoyed at household habits or not having done something promised, but they were *fighting*. About *Elsa*. And Mom swore. Mom never swore. Dad didn't swear much either, except during Iowa football games, driving home with hot food in the car, and after extremely bad days at work.

I concluded one of two things in that instant: Mom and Dad were getting a divorce, or we were getting rid of Elsa.

I looked at Sister for guidance. Her eyes were as wide as mine, but she didn't come to the cataclysmic conclusions that would haunt my dreams for weeks. I dared to say the

D-word out loud. "They're not going to get a divorce, are they?"

Sister hesitated but shook her head. "They're just fighting, that's all."

"But they never fight."

She shrugged her shoulders but didn't exude the confidence to convince me that all would be well.

We could hear no more voices from upstairs. Elsa had not come downstairs with us, so I feared for her safety. Our dogs seemed to disappear on me. I couldn't bear the thought of Elsa being with me one second, and then gone the next.

We dared to go back upstairs; the unsettling silence told us we would not interrupt the argument. Mom sat in the living room, with a cigarette burning in her ashtray, lips pursed, stabbing her needle through the fabric in her embroidery hoop. Elsa sat with her side leaning up against Dad's vacant chair, resting on her hip like always. When she saw us, she gave us a goofy smile, but her eyes remained in their puppy-dog state as if she knew she was the cause of the discontent.

Mom looked too prickly to approach—we were not an affectionate family anyway. We never gave hugs and kisses or said, "I love you." We barely uttered, "Good job," usually pointing out that which didn't succeed more than high-fiving successes. With Elsa, I lavished kisses and hugs upon her daily, even telling her how much I loved her. As much as I wanted to do that, I didn't want to anger Mom by hugging the dog, since such affection was precisely what caused this apocalyptic fight.

After sitting in the living room for a few awkward moments, we made ourselves scarce. Elsa followed us out of the room. I didn't want her out of my sight.

I hugged Elsa and whispered to her, "Don't worry. It's not your fault."

Later that afternoon, Dad was much more attentive to Mom, his demeanor sensitive and apologetic. He even spoke with a light, cautious tone that I had never heard before, like a scene from *Invasion of the Body Snatchers*. While we were all gathered in the living room, Dad said to Mom, "I'm sorry I pay more attention to the dog." Mom's face softened.

Sister butted in. "How can you resist this face?" She draped her arm around Elsa and put her cheek next to Elsa's furry one. I joined in on the other side, sandwiching Elsa's face between our cheeks.

I think we all smiled and laughed, like a *Brady Bunch* episode. At least that's how I ended the conflict at that moment.

Just that one fight shifted the axis on our ever-predictable household, as if we had opened Pandora's box. Now that such an argument had happened once, could it happen again?

I went to bed that night still replaying the day's events. I worried about a lot as a child: getting a sliver, skinning my knee at recess, throwing up, Elsa running away, losing Little Animal, missing Barbie accessories, Grumpy Bear's mental state, tornadoes, spiders in my room, finding a seat on the abhorrent school bus, getting an answer wrong on a test… some of these fears sprung from traumatic events, like when I skinned my knee on the playground and then fainted in front of my third grade class. Yet my hypersensitive mind triggered panic alarms over relatively benign threats that cemented in my memory, ready to flare up at any reminder.

I would write about my parents' fight at school, when the teacher told us to write about the unhappiest day of fifth grade.

I eventually asked Mom for reassurance, because as a fifth grader, Mom had never proven herself wrong except with the whole ignore-them-and-they'll-stop-teasing-you bit. She had so far been right about my eyesight: thanks to *Little House on the Prairie*, I feared I'd go blind like Mary because I had scarlet fever and that's what caused Mary's blindness. (Years later I would learn that dedicated people with the same obsession with everything *Little House on the Prairie* would research and discover that scarlet fever didn't cause Mary's blindness. Viral meningoencephalitis caused the fever, head pains, and stroke. Mary regained her mobility, but never her eyesight. If only I had known this when I was six for it would have saved me years of worry.) Mom told me every time that episode aired, "You had penicillin. Mary didn't. You won't go blind." This would ease my fears until the next time I saw the episode.

To end my inexhaustible worry, I asked Mom if she was divorcing Dad. She stifled a laugh when she saw the look on my face, probably my there's-a-spider-in-my-room face or I-have-a-sliver face or Mary-is-screaming-for-Pa-when-she-woke-up-and-couldn't-see face. "No, why would you ask that?"

"Because you were mad about Elsa."

Mom nodded, the kind of nod only moms can give when they understand their children's bizarre behavior. "No, we are not getting a divorce. Couples don't always agree. You fight with Sister all the time, but she's still your family."

I didn't respond, thinking that might not have been the best example to give me.

Mom locked eyes with me. "Right?"

I nodded. "I guess."

"Now go play. Stop worrying. Your dad and I are not getting divorced."

Although I still suffered from flashes of insecurity about that fight, its intensity weakened, its strength zapped, either from time or replaced with other worries.

I scoffed whenever Mom said Sister was the sensitive one, which I heard a thousand times—literally—throughout my childhood *and* adulthood. Sister was the moody one. *I* was the sensitive one.

ELSA MCNUGGET

Thanks to my food issues, Elsa discovered Chicken McNuggets and declared it one of her favorite foods.

I refused to eat McDonald's cheeseburgers after throwing them up in fifth grade (this was something that I would carry throughout my life—if I threw it up, I would never eat it again). We were not allowed to special order any fast-food meal—for reasons unknown, my parents said special ordering fast food would mess up the entire order. I ate only fries on those rare occasions we ate at McDonald's because I couldn't stomach the onions after seeing them float in the toilet. I couldn't order the Filet-O-Fish because who puts cheese on fish?

And then I discovered Chicken McNuggets. According to the internet, McNuggets had been available since 1983. I threw up my cheeseburger in 1986. Perhaps our home-made meals and severe supper routine prohibited me from finding these precious little pressed chicken chunks sooner. Maybe South Dakota didn't get them until later. I'll never know. But I first discovered them on our way to Iowa to visit my grandparents.

Elsa loved going to Iowa, probably because other than the vet, she rarely went for rides. She always sat near my feet since I was the shortest. We drove a blue Jimmy then; we would outgrow it, trading it in for a blue minivan when I was in junior high. The Jimmy provided little space for Elsa to sit comfortably. For reasons only she could tell, she perched herself on the padded armrest next to my window, squeezing herself uncomfortably between the window and my bony shoulder. Otherwise, she slept on the floor by my feet.

Just outside of Des Moines, Dad stopped at McDonald's, marking our last 60 miles before we arrived at our grandparents' town. Other than driving through Sioux City and Des Moines, McDonald's was the only excitement in our interstate drive. A few months after my vomiting trauma, I ordered the unknown entity that was the Chicken McNugget.

Elsa stared at me while I ate, interested in the new finger food that was designed perfectly for picky eaters. Since they weren't messy, I shared half of one with Elsa. She gobbled it up and asked for seconds. Then thirds. Out of the six McNuggets, I ate only two. Those nuggets made her so happy; I didn't mind being hungry.

The next time, I gave all six to Elsa.

Elsa knew what those Golden Arches meant. It wasn't just the rest stop where she stretched her legs and peed. She knew lunch was some greasy chicken chunks.

I don't know how many trips we took before my parents realized I was back to eating only fries. Maybe when we arrived at my grandma's house, I asked for something to eat right away because I was starving. Maybe I said something while we were still in the car. But they caved. Dad bought Elsa her own order of McNuggets.

Since Elsa devoured her six long before I had my six eaten, she usually ended up eating a ten piece before ten pieces were a thing. I only ate three or four (okay, maybe two) and gave the rest to her.

Even when we were at home, Dad ordered Elsa her own McNuggets.

McNuggets remained Elsa's favorite. KFC might have trumped McNuggets, but she didn't receive her own piece of chicken out of the bucket, just table scraps. Having her own little box of McNuggets elevated the experience— those were just for her. As much as she loved licking Taco Bell taco wrappers or shoving her nose into a French fry container, those were still leftovers. She knew all those McNuggets were meant for her.

My college friend loved her dog (almost) as much as I loved Elsa, so she understood my penchant for treating dogs like spoiled babies. She stayed with me one weekend while my parents went to Iowa for a class reunion. Being the geeks that we were, we planned no party or wild adventure. We watched classic Eighties movies, ate pizza (I gave Elsa all my pepperoni), and fantasized about how much fun we would have upon our return to college. We only left the house to take Elsa for a ride. First around the loop, a downtown gathering place for teenagers who have nothing better to do, and then to the McDonald's drive-thru for some Chicken McNuggets.

We drove my friend's car, whose four-door design was easier for Elsa.

Dad had made wooden steps for Elsa. Now ten years old, Elsa was not mobile enough to jump in and out of cars without assistance. Her geriatric out-of-shape body required stairs to climb into cars. My friend and I struggled with the heavy steps, both of us together having the arm strength of a toddler. Elsa smiled and panted in the backseat while we drove around the loop. She loved the window she had all to herself, something our minivan didn't allow. She stuck her nose out into the summer night air, like a girl letting the wind whip through her hair. Elsa knew what to expect once she saw those Golden Arches.

Neither of us ordered anything for ourselves since we had snacked most of the night. It was dark already that August night, well past Elsa's bedtime. After we bought her McNuggets, I tucked a napkin into her collar and took a picture of her panting, a girls' night out of debauchery. I handed her a couple of McNuggets on the way home because it's more fun to eat in the car. Getting out of the car was just as laborious as getting in, but she had much more giddy-up in her step now with the McNuggets.

Animals are simple in their wants, wants I can easily fulfill. They don't criticize what you give them. They don't lecture you on logic or practicality or purpose or consequences. The nonverbal communication between a human and her pet needs no words, only a soulful understanding that you are one, sharing the same space—or McNuggets—with the same goal: happiness.

BUS BOYFRIEND

Elsa became my most important confidant in seventh and eighth grade. My friends didn't live within walking distance, so I rarely saw them outside school. If I didn't have lunch with them, we had little time for talking, especially since I rode the bus, eliminating those precious free minutes before and after school. I had zero social life until the end of eighth grade; I spent much of my time in my room, hiding from Sister's drama. The world was ending daily by her interpretation of events, so my room became my pink utopia. Once we moved to our split-foyer house, Mom finally allowed me to have my precious pink bedroom: pale dusty rose walls with carpet to match and even a pink satin comforter I had coveted for years. I preferred solitude to socialization: anything I told Sister went back to Mom; anything I told Mom, she told Sister, as if a committee needed to meet to deal with my pathetic problems. (All problems were categorized as pathetic if my sister wasn't the one experiencing them.)

I learned the less I shared, the better off I was. Revealing intimate details of my life or my worries with anyone drained me of all energy; the fallout rarely produced a positive result, mostly minimizing concerns that were paramount to me as a teenager. I sought out Elsa instead. She would never tell. Or criticize. Or use it against me later. She was a witness to my first kiss and never told a soul.

I was in seventh grade, and he was in eighth. I never saw him at school, but we rode the same bus. In those days, school buses didn't go to junior highs, so we had to rely on the city bus for transportation. School buses were hell on wheels, but city buses were what would happen to Hell if Hell had a zombie apocalypse that stranded everyone at the DMV. One day he just started talking to me when the bus emptied out of other students. Because the bus picked me up and dropped me off at the corner, the west side of our backyard was visible, giving me a view of Elsa standing at the chain-link fence, waiting for me. I always waved to her as I stepped off the bus, unaware that others might find that odd or crazy or childish (I still wave at my pets).

This served as a conversation starter between me and Bus Boyfriend.

"Why do you always wave to your dog when you get off the bus?"

"Why wouldn't I?"

I imagine my face lit up at the mention of Elsa, an easy icebreaker for an awkward boy to an introverted girl. Later that night, I realized he must have been watching me to notice my interactions with Elsa. That meant he liked me, right? Elsa neither confirmed nor denied my theory.

That hellacious bus ride home became my favorite part of the day. For whatever reason, he didn't ride the bus in the mornings. I had somebody I could talk to on that meandering ride, although I don't think we talked about anything all that important. Junior high small talk is inconsequential yet life-changing, one of the many paradoxes that exist in the confusing lives of teens. We had little in common except dogs. He had some retriever/collie mix with a name I cannot recall.

He even dared to move from his seat across from me to sit right next to me, our legs intermittently touching during the bumpy ride. We never exchanged phone numbers.

We were bus dating, if that was a thing.

Bus Boyfriend had a dog and I had a dog, so we agreed to meet in the park one day, which was just a block from my house. I chose a day when Sister didn't work; I could bet on her having a meltdown, so no one would question why I wanted to get out of the house and walk the dog. It saved both me and Elsa from the yelling and the tears and the minimization of any problem I had because I couldn't possibly understand Sister's Big Girl Problems.

The dreary spring day almost gave me a reason to bail. The sun had disappeared behind a gray sky that threatened to mist. Upon entering the house and hearing the same shit drama of friends and boyfriends and mean girls and dance teams and rotten teachers and the unfairness of the world, I asked Elsa, "You want to go for a walk?"

Her eyes said yes as she bounced up and down. I put on her leash, and we walked out the front door, probably unnoticed.

I met Bus Boyfriend on the other side of the park, just as planned. We introduced our dogs to one other; after sniffing each other's butt, they went their separate ways, pulling our arms in opposite directions as if they knew this coupling would not last. After the prerequisite awkwardness of small talk, we were alone for the first time, at least from a human factor. Elsa tugged on the leash as she walked around me as far as she could go, investigating the grass. His dog did the same. Our height difference dwarfed me—I felt like a little kid when I stood next to him, which might have prompted Bus Boyfriend to sit on top of a picnic table. I plopped down next to him, attempting to appear flippant about the magnitude of our bus dating. I knew he was going to kiss me when I sat next to him. Yet did I want that to happen? Part of me did, so that I could get it over with, to gain experience, to shed my juvenile skin. But the other part of me worried what would happen after—would it change our current status of bus dating and if so, to what? As the silent minutes stretched on, I decided to leave. Just as I said, "I better go," he leaned over and kissed me.

No bells sounded in my head, just a peculiar mushiness on my lips that was neither pleasant nor life changing. Certainly not what my V.C. Andrews books had promised. We said nothing after our kiss, instead running in opposite directions, our dogs leading the way. Elsa and I sprinted all the way through the park to the street.

My first kiss gave me an excitement in a life that felt devoid of such social intensity, yet I concluded that kiss didn't change my life the way I had anticipated. But I felt different, more mature, as if I had stepped into a time machine and come out the other side years into the future. I cherished having such a sacred secret that neither Mom nor Sister knew. No one could minimize or judge my experience because no one else knew about it. Only Elsa, who didn't judge or tell.

I never told anyone about my kiss that day, yet I analyzed it at length with Elsa, especially when Bus Boyfriend didn't show up on the bus for days, which relieved me of stressful awkwardness. When he finally did, we no longer sat next to each other, but across from each other, acting like the other didn't exist.

The only part I regretted was his proximity. Since I had no friends within walking distance, a boyfriend who lived just past the park maybe would have freed me from the confines of the house. And I could have even taken Elsa with me.

Six years later, the summer between my freshman and sophomore year of college, Bus Boyfriend would appear on my doorstep to deliver a pizza. I stood flabbergasted in the doorway when I saw him, pizza in hand, waiting for the cash that my own hand gripped. Elsa stood at the corner of the banister, barking as she stuck her head through the spindles, her normal spot during all pizza deliveries. She could see the door from her position and the person at the door could easily see her, a nice line of protection in case a serial killer happened to knock. I sensed a peculiarity in Elsa's low bark-growl, as if she remembered him and didn't approve or even sought a little vengeance.

Although Bus Boyfriend remained stoic as I handed him my money, his eyes flickered with recognition. If he couldn't recognize me, he surely remembered my house. And the dog that looked like a wolf.

I couldn't shut the door fast enough.

My friend and I suffered from a giggling fit as I tried to tell her my story between snorts of laughter. We plopped on the floor with Elsa, who munched on the pepperoni I had peeled off my pizza and given to her. Elsa seemed to share the details of my first kiss as she sat next to me, just like one of the girls.

I wonder how she would have told the story.

VET DREAMS

My first career choice: a Solid Gold dancer. *Solid Gold* was a hit in the early Eighties. I don't remember the premise of the show, only that a group of girls, who typically wore gold, danced throughout to glitzy choreography (like an early Eighties' version of the Fly Girls on *In Living Color*). When I was four, I wanted to wear heels and dance to popular music while donning sparkly costumes.

I had little understanding of trendy music and dance styles, not to mention that *Solid Gold*'s popularity would not last more than a couple of years, dying out with the last remnants of disco-like pop music, long before I ever earned a paycheck.

That didn't matter much anyway. I grew up in a household where something like dance was considered a hobby, not a career.

I was heavily influenced by television, my small square window into the world beyond my house and school. After I fell in love with *Little House on the Prairie*, I wanted to write about my life. Laura Ingalls Wilder lived in South Dakota;

other than Bob Barker, I knew no famous person from the state. Despite my begging to visit DeSmet (which was only 90 miles away), I would not see it until after my own son was born. Sister warned me the books were nothing like the show—Pa was no Michael Landon. I didn't read the books until later but knowing that a fictional Albert could have never burned down a fictional blind school never weakened the story for me. It was the idea that Laura Ingalls Wilder existed and because of her and her books, *Little House on the Prairie* existed. I could write stories about my life. I imagined a TV series and wondered who would play the parts. But writing also fell under the category of hobby, not career. If I became a teacher, that would leave me summers to write. If Laura could do it, so could I. (If only I had known that Laura's teaching career was short-lived and the sole purpose was to fund Mary's college education and that Laura was in her early sixties when she began writing her books.)

I played school all the time; it looked fun to be a teacher, at least in the Eighties when children were more well-behaved than today's children. (Ornery kids existed, but the outright defiance and swearing and challenging a teacher's every rule wasn't the norm.) My stuffed animals behaved impeccably, sat quietly, and raised their hands to ask insightful questions. They were talented in art and music too (I banished PE from my school). Once I grew out of playing teacher, I abandoned the idea for new television influences I discovered.

LA Law inspired me to become a lawyer. I wanted Grace VanOwen's job as a prosecutor but wanted to dress like Abigail Perkins because Grace wore too many navy and neutral tones and button-down dresses with huge shoulder pads. (I also preferred Abby's spunky curly hair to Grace's boring shoulder-length blond straight hair with the infinitely dark roots.)

Then after watching *When Rabbit Howls*, a TV movie based on a true story starring Shelley Long, I wanted to be a psychiatrist who specialized in multiple personality disorder. Mom bought the book for me at Waldenbooks, and I finished it in a day. (Good thing I abandoned that idea since the mass diagnosis of multiple personality disorder was based on the hoax that was Sybil, which I didn't discover until my thirties.)

I became addicted to TV movies based on true stories, thanks to Lifetime, which played such movies nonstop: *The Burning Bed*, *The Tracey Thurman Story*, *A Killing in a Small Town*, *The Karen Carpenter Story*, and later *The Betty Broderick Story* and *In the Best of Families: Marriage, Pride, and Madness*. This then led me to their books, mostly true crime although any true story would do. *Helter Skelter* sat on our bookshelves downstairs, I found *The Boston Strangler* and *In Cold Blood* at a garage sale and began reading books about Marilyn Monroe. While a prosecutor still sounded fun, I wanted to be a forensic psychiatrist and profile serial killers. Such a career would provide plenty of material for writing books.

In ninth grade, English class became my favorite subject. My teacher, Mrs. Schmitz, impressed me with her wit and passion and application of the material (she shared her own written essays for assignment examples, which no teacher had ever done before—she would be the only teacher I ever had who did this until my college creative writing class).

And she told us that no one was allowed to bother her on Thursday nights because *LA Law* was her favorite show. She was in love with Jimmy Smits. (I preferred Jimmy Smits over Harry Hamlin, too, who I could only see as Perseus.)

Teacher circled itself back to a possible career. And English was now my favorite subject.

Mom responded to my career indecision by steering me in the direction of veterinarian. Since I loved animals so much, a career as a vet made sense. Mom pointed out problems with my other career interests:

Lawyers did not have the exciting careers portrayed on *LA Law*. In the Midwest, I'd be lucky to ever partake in a murder trial. A majority of the job was paperwork. (I thought secretly I could move to California, but wisely kept this to myself.) Mom's idea of paperwork was my idea of research and writing—building a narrative out of a crime. Plus, I could specialize in litigating, not the kind of lawyer like Stuart Markowitz who rarely entered a courtroom.

Forensic psychiatrists were too much of a novelty, so it would be difficult for me to find a job. What else would I do with such a degree?

Teacher was okay, but wouldn't it be better to be a math teacher? (My family valued the sciences more than the arts, which all arts were just hobbies, not careers.)

As for a writer, see above. Journalism was acceptable though.

Mom declared a vet was a viable career choice. I pointed out problems with that:

I fainted at the sight of blood and needles, so how would I administer shots to animals? And wouldn't that require me to operate on animals, too? I couldn't handle simple first aid for a paper cut (and yes, when I got a paper cut, I needed first aid). The Invisible Man we found at a garage sale made me nauseous. Sister enjoyed taking all his organs out, but I didn't. Halloween skeletons were even pushing it. In health class, I looked at the floor much of the time. The X-ray footage of eating and swallowing even made me woozy— and I never wanted to eat again.

As much as I loved animals, I wasn't fond of bodily fluids. Vomit especially. Doggie drool I could handle, and I did fetch Barbie shoes out of Elsa's poop. I never babysat. Lacking experience in poop and spit up, a vet was a far-fetched idea.

While I didn't have much fear regarding dogs and cats, I was hesitant around anything that could bite or scratch me or trample me. I had never been around livestock nor up close to wild animals like raccoons or squirrels and had no interest in the reptile community.

But most of all, how could I put any animal to sleep? Even if they were suffering, I couldn't imagine that I would have to kill beloved dogs and cats as part of my career.

Mom didn't find my arguments strong. She was the one who wanted to be an OB/GYN but did the Seventies' thing by becoming a wife and mother. Her childhood would have been a sound upbringing for a future vet. I didn't raise bunnies or guinea pigs or trained ponies or dogs or nursed sickly farm cats or butchered chickens every day like she did. Collecting stuffed animals and thinking they were real didn't qualify as good life experience.

I had to leave the living room when Mom tended to a boil on Elsa's side, yet Mom remained relentless, believing a veterinarian was my future. It wasn't like I was a senior in high school. I was only in ninth grade, not thinking about the future except longing to be thirty so I could make my own decisions and have lives like the characters on *thirtysomething*. I spent more time worrying about friends and potential boyfriends and all I felt I was missing out on while Mom wanted to plan my future. She cornered me one afternoon. "Is your fainting problem holding you back?"

That's how we referred to it: *my fainting problem*.

"What do you mean?" I had no idea the context of the question. Of course my fainting problem held me back. I avoided situations that could result in bleeding injuries or ripped nails that tore my cuticles and bled. I worried about stuff that could happen, that I had no control over, like bloody noses and appendicitis.

Before the internet and WebMD, Mom looked up every ailment in her *Gray's Anatomy* book and diagnosed whatever symptoms we presented, knowing exactly if we needed to see a doctor or not. "I could take you to a psychologist for desensitization."

Desensitization. Sounded scary. Once Mom explained what it was, I put it into terms that made sense to me. "I'm scared of spiders. So they would put me in a room with a bunch of spiders so that I wouldn't be scared of them anymore?" Just the thought gave me the heebie-jeebies.

Mom backpedaled. "Not exactly. But they would expose you to needles and such so they wouldn't bother you anymore."

My insides screamed no, but to placate my mother, I said, "Let me think about it."

I did love animals, but I knew I could never be their nurse or doctor. I took the easy way out. A few days later, I told Mom, "I would never be able to accept that a part of my job would be putting dogs and cats to sleep." Which was completely true.

Mom accepted that.

I ended up an English teacher. I could have never become a vet, although I wish I would have become a lawyer (a marriage counselor would confirm that I argued like a lawyer) or a forensic psychiatrist. If you're reading this, then my dream of emulating Laura Ingalls Wilder came true, so I must have made the right choice. (And Mom, I'm writing about animals, so it all worked out in the end).

THE WEIGHT OF IT

Elsa was a social eater.

Elsa's favorite time of day was prime time television. Not only were we all gathered in the living room to watch *The Wonder Years* or *Roseanne*, but my parents were notorious snackers.

Mom ate a bowl of cereal for breakfast—whatever light-sugary goodness sat in the cupboard, like Frosted Flakes, Alphabits, or Corn Pops. She didn't touch our Cookie Crisp while we didn't touch her Grape Nuts. She followed that with a glass of milk, then drank coffee until she switched to weak instant iced tea midmorning. For lunch, she would grab something quick and easy—maybe an Oscar Mayer ham sandwich or nothing at all.

Dad's breakfast consisted of coffee. Every morning, he made himself a peanut butter sandwich to bring to work. Both Mom and Dad saved up all their caloric intake for supper and nighttime snacks.

Cheetos always sat in our cupboards (but never Doritos). Apples chilled in our fridge. Junk food mixed with healthy options throughout the kitchen. Baked goods, salads, left-overs, Twinkies or Ho Hos…Mom loved Twizzlers and Dad loved EL Fudge cookies.

Elsa adored the smorgasbord of treats, sampling a bit from everyone, with Cheetos her favorite (says every dog everywhere).

Even Elsa's own treats turned into social experiments as I conducted taste tests with her. I'd tell her to sit while I set out multiple treats in front of her. When her butt raised from the floor just a bit, I'd say, "Wait," so she sat until I gave her instructions. She'd sniff and select the one she wanted. In the Eighties and early Nineties, Milk Bone variety boxes contained four flavors: milk, chicken, beef, and vegetable. Elsa chose the chicken and beef flavors first all the time. The vegetable was her least favorite (I don't think that's even a flavor offered anymore). She always chose Meaty Bones over Milk Bones, then buried them for later, placing the flat side edge against the basement mopboards—the same deep reddish-brown of Meaty Bones (dogs can't be completely colorblind, considering we could barely see the bone that blended in seamlessly with the mopboard). I wanted to do my eighth-grade science project on Elsa, but my teacher said I couldn't if I didn't have a bigger sampling of dogs.

Once the vet told Mom that Elsa was overweight, I wondered if it was my fault.

In eighth grade, I needed Elsa to win back some control. She was my only friend at the table. I paid her in meat.

During supper, I became Sister's verbal punching bag. My life was minimized, my problems pathetic, my existence questionable while my sister unleased all her hatred of the world at the table, some of it directed at me. Mom refused to intervene, telling me, "It makes her feel better to get everything off her chest."

That was when I decided to become a vegetarian.

I had been picking pepperoni off my pizza for years, giving it to Elsa (it was blasphemous to ask for cheese pizza). I hated ham and didn't enjoy bacon or sausage. We rarely ate chicken because Mom had spent her childhood plucking feathers from dead chickens and wanted no part preparing chicken meals as an adult. Ninety-nine percent of our meals were beef: Swiss steak, roast, beef and noodles, spaghetti and meatballs, lasagna, pizza burgers, goulash, steak, hamburgers, chili stew, and the occasional meatloaf. Every night I'd find another dead animal on my plate. I no longer wanted to eat anything that used to have a face.

Announcing my new vegetarian status would not have been acceptable. (Yet somehow my sister's atrocious table talk assault was.) The only ally I had during suppertime was Elsa. She gladly helped me become a vegetarian, unbeknownst to my family.

Since I was invisible, I cut up my Swiss steak and gave each piece to Elsa. I didn't even try to be sneaky. Instead of bringing the fork to my mouth, I picked up the meaty bit covered in cream of mushroom soup and handed it to her. No one noticed as everyone kept their eyes on their own plate while Sister's diatribe about life's unfairness lasted throughout the meal. I ate my mashed potatoes and gravy in between Elsa's bites of Swiss steak. My first meat-free supper at that table. And no one noticed.

In the sanctity of my room, I basked in my glorious victory in a battle that no one even knew I was fighting. My only wound was my invisibility.

I was in college before I ever ate a hamburger again at home. We rarely shared bread and condiments with Elsa. Instead, I asked for a hot dog, much smaller and probably not made of just meat. I abhorred steak, which easily went to Elsa. I picked meat out of my stew, left a pile of hamburger on my plate from goulash or lasagna, only took meatballs for the sole purpose of saving them for Elsa, and scraped off the top of the baked ketchup from the meatloaf before giving her the rest. Chili was the only beef I remember consuming at the table.

(For full disclosure, my idea of vegetarian was random. I ate leftover beef and noodles or a cold roast beef sandwich the next day at lunch. I usually ordered chicken or fish from fast food places and stopped eating hot KFC but would eat it cold the next day, sharing most of it with Elsa. I just refused all meat at the table when I had to sit next to Nurse Ratched.)

Elsa's weight appeared to balloon after that, although her nighttime snacking with my parents also factored into all that weight gain.

My preconceived (and pathetic) win had dire consequences for me four years later. When I was a senior in high school and felt I had zero control over anything in my life, I stopped eating. Everything. Not just meat and not just at the table.

BESTIES & BOYS

Once I entered junior high, my existence was a lonely one.

I relied on Elsa, perhaps too much.

I shared everything with her (mostly food) and ran around with her outside on nice days and escaped on afternoon walks (I was a fair weather outside friend).

I even listed Elsa as one of my friends in a sixth-grade writing project. I described her as *nice, cute, pretty, and sincere.*

In junior high and then high school, my fierce devotion to Elsa became obvious to my friends even if they never came to my house. They said I treated her like a baby, like she was more than just a pet. I never cared if people made fun of me for it.

Enter Evan, who lived down the block from me and sat behind me in sixth grade.

Smart and a bit geeky, Evan's biggest weakness was his desire to be popular. I never bothered with such triteness; I befriended misfits and geeks and dorky girls who didn't care about fitting in with the popular kids. Evan spent most of sixth grade pulling my hair that would sometimes rest on his desk. Mom declared that any boy who pulled my hair liked me. She was probably right, but in my sixth-grade mind, boys were gross.

Because Evan walked past my house every day to school, he saw Elsa frequently in our yard. Although not much of a barker, she always barked at Evan. I had told Elsa all about Evan and gave her the okay to bark at him.

Evan asked me one day, "What's wrong with your dog? She always barks at me."

"There's nothing wrong with Elsa. Maybe it's you!"

It didn't help when I presented a poster about Elsa for a school assignment. Gluing pictures and applying glitter, I created a collage all about my beloved dog. The assignment involved developing a character. Everyone else chose people, either family members or celebrities. My teacher complimented me on my creativity, for characters didn't have to be human. Evan teased me about my poster. I told him he couldn't possibly understand because he didn't have a dog. He threatened to shoot out Elsa's kneecaps in various horrific scenarios. I called him a monster.

When I told Mom, she doubled down on her theory that Evan liked me. "He's just getting under your skin when he says stuff about Elsa. That's how boys flirt."

Boys were gross *and* stupid.

In junior high, boys were no longer gross, just stupid. When my best friend gave me a locket for my birthday, I put Elsa's picture inside it. Her little face smiled at whoever opened the gold heart. From the inside of my junior high locker, Elsa greeted me at school, an adorable picture of her in the foyer, with one leg draped over the edge of the stairs (I would hang up a similar picture of her in my high school locker, but that one had her favorite toy, Moo Moo Cow Cow, next to her). When I had to bring in a family picture to write about for English class, I couldn't find one with all five of us. I used a professional one that we had taken the year before. (Mom didn't believe in taking professional family photos with pets.) Then I cut out Elsa from a picture of her sitting on a rocking chair and taped her off to the side as though she posed in the picture with us.

One friend told me, "We love our pets, Julie. Just not like you do."

My parents demanded any boy who asked us out—and it had to be a date, not just a bunch of people hanging out because my mother still thought it was 1961—to come to the door and meet them. Most boys stood awkwardly in the foyer, counting down the seconds introductions would take to get the hell out of there. Elsa slowed the process at times. She took her spot at the corner, wedged between the end table and the wall, stuck her head between the banister, and barked. Sometimes her bark sounded like a greeting, other times a threat. My first boyfriend worried more about my dog's approval than my parents' approval. "Does your dog bark like that to everyone who comes over?"

I shrugged. "Sometimes."

He said, "Dogs love me. All other dogs I've been around never bark at me."

Elsa always smelled the losers from the keepers. (Too bad I didn't pay attention to her instinct.)

Evan re-entered my life in high school because we saw each other twice a day in chemistry and then Spanish. Evan picked up where we had left off. "I think you're overfeeding Elsa. She looks a lot bigger than she used to."

"She's just husky. There's more of her to love."

By this time, Mom had received yearly lectures from the vet about Elsa's weight. My parents even watched their own nighttime snacking. To accommodate Elsa's diet, we placed a bowl of Kibbles 'N Bits in the living room, hoping she would munch on that while Dad ate Cheetos. Dad created hors d'oeuvres out of her kibbles, shoving the little red soft cylinder pieces into the holes in the crunchy bits. Elsa liked eating her dog food that way, but nothing could replace beloved Cheetos.

We nicknamed her Bear, since her girth had grown, with the extra weight around her neck shortening the appearance of her snout. I covered Elsa's ears if a friend said something about her weight, then whispered, "We don't talk about it in front of her."

My best friend also thought Evan was in love with me. The only remotely cool thing about me was that I was on the dance team. (My love of dance trumped my distaste for high school cliques of any kind.) My best friend was a geeky misfit; we shared the same brain. While I acted like a geek, I didn't look like a geek, making it difficult to place me into a Breakfast Club category. I remained in my own little world. Evan's wish had come true: he hung out with some of the worst pricks at school and dressed in preppy clothes, pairing Ralph Lauren polo shirts with Girbaud jeans. He joined the golf team (cool) but was vice-president of the foreign language club (uncool). If he did like me, he never asked me out, probably because I would destroy his dreams of reaching the highest pinnacle of preppydom.

But the endless teasing about Elsa never stopped. "There's something wrong with your dog. She's always barking at me."

"I told her you say horrible things about her."

"I don't say mean things about her."

"You threaten to shoot her kneecaps."

Evan laughed. "You'd think I'd actually shoot your dog?"

"It's not even nice to joke about such a thing."

Up until Evan noticed a strange car in my driveway and figured out I had a boyfriend who attended another high school in town, the only two topics of conversation included Elsa and our complaints about chemistry class. He teased me about my boyfriend because boys were still stupid. I never believed he liked me until one morning when he said to me, "I hope he treats you well. You deserve to be with somebody nice."

I preferred the days when he made fun of Elsa.

I insisted upon taking my senior pictures with Elsa. Mom didn't agree, but surprisingly relented since our senior picture package included an outdoor setting. I posed for my outdoor pictures at the Falls, a rocky waterfall park with plenty of picture possibilities (in the Nineties, people still predominantly took studio shots, whereas now it's odd to even have studio pictures.)

I wanted to match Elsa's black and gray fur, so I wore a white hat with a black ribbon around it and paired that with white shorts and a black and white striped shirt. The humidity of the morning summer air straightened all my hot-rolled curls. The photographer took three poses with Elsa, only one of which turned out fabulous. I'm sitting on a stone wall and Elsa is standing next to me. My arm rests around her neck and she looks perky at the camera. I only wish I had worn my hat for that pose.

I had fulfilled one dream—senior pictures with Elsa. Now I just needed to have her as my flower girl at my wedding and my life would be complete.

Evan and I exchanged senior pictures at the end of the school year. Mom didn't allow me to order wallets of my picture with Elsa. I wish I would have because that was the pose Evan deserved most. Instead, I settled for my red dress studio pose. His was a faraway outdoor shot with him leaning on an arched doorway. On the back, he wrote well wishes for the future. He closed it with this: *And by the way, I do think you have a nice dog.*

Fun fact: Evan became a Doctor of Veterinary Medicine, an odd choice since I never heard him speak lovingly of animals and as far as I knew, he never owned a pet.

BLESSED IS THEE

My favorite strangers in the world: those on television who are walking through flooded areas after hurricanes with dogs on their shoulders, cat kennels over their heads, or dogs sitting in boats. I root for those people, the ones who guaranteed their pets aren't left behind during natural disasters.

I always make sure my babies are safely in the basement when tornado sirens blare.

I'm so thankful that it's never come to worse.

My junior year of high school, I took American Studies, a two-period class that combined American literature with American history. It became my favorite class. That was the same year *Schindler's List* premiered, and my teachers coordinated a field trip to the movie theater so the junior class could watch it.

I knew the Holocaust well, thanks to Anne Frank's diary, which I read in sixth grade. Mom bought me a diary that Christmas, a small dark brown one with a lock. But I stopped journaling when I realized that all I wrote about was my mean sister, childish friend fights, and my invisibility. My experiences contained none of the profundity of Anne Frank's, not to mention she called her diary Kitty and it felt sacrilegious to copy such cuteness.

I had also read *Alicia*, a Holocaust survivor's memoir, which was densely packed with details. I couldn't imagine the horror, the fear, the day-to-day nightmares that Europe's Jews endured (as well as all the other groups of people the Nazis targeted). I always wondered if in a past life I had perished during the Holocaust, for I felt connected to their experiences even though I had never faced any such trauma in my own life.

The Holocaust brought me much needed perspective in what I perceived to be my pathetic existence.

I sat entranced throughout *Schindler's List*, near tears many times, while my friends ate and drank their snacks and whispered to each other. For all the horrifying scenes in *Schindler's List*, the one that upset me the most appeared benign on the surface: the Nazis dividing up all the Jews' belongings who arrived in Auschwitz. The mountains of shoes, the piles of valuables, the discarded family photographs, and the empty suitcases that once held such worldly treasures—*we* had shoes, and family keepsakes, and oh so many pictures. I could see my family's stuff in those piles as I watched people in the movie lose everything, including their lives. Everything was being taken from them by other human beings. It was as if they never existed.

I wondered what would have happened to my mom and dad and sister and me had we been European Jews during that time. I would have been separated from Dad immediately, perhaps never to know what happened to him. Mom,

Sister, and I would have tried to stay together, but would we have been able to? Would Mom's strength have kept us alive, or would she have crumbled, refusing to survive if that meant hiding in the sewers or lying under corpses?

When I came home from school, I found Mom sitting in the living room, drinking iced tea, her right leg flung over the arm of her rocker recliner. Before she could even ask me about the movie, I said, "What would we have done had we been Jewish during the Holocaust?"

Mom placed her glass on the coaster. Without deliberation she said, "We would have left long before they had a chance to round us up."

My mother, so ready to move? Mom didn't like to go anywhere, not even to my grandparents' houses. We never went on vacation, yet she was willing to start a new life elsewhere—in a foreign land where she might not even speak the language?

"How?"

"Whatever it takes," she said and picked up her lotion, rubbing it into her hands.

"We'd leave everything behind?" I don't know if I was challenging my homebody of a mother or trying to rationalize within myself that whatever it takes meant *whatever it takes*.

"Stuff is replaceable. Our lives are not."

I grappled with this statement, which came from a woman who clipped newspaper articles, who saved boxes of old family knickknacks like school patches and receipts, and who had kept her Beatles records in pristine condition. If she was willing to ditch all her stuff, that meant Grumpy Bear and Barbie were headed for the dumpster.

Then I looked at Elsa, who was snoring on the living room floor in front of the windows, a beam of sunshine turning her gray hair to silver. Her fur rose and fell with every snore. Mom followed my gaze.

"What about Elsa?" My voice was barely audible.

"We couldn't take her with us." Mom's tone lacked sentimentality, a matter-of-fact statement that offered no remorse if we had to face such a dire situation.

"So, what, we'd just leave her?" Panic rose from my stomach, as if this fictitious scenario could happen to us tomorrow.

"You do what you have to do to survive."

The reality of her words shattered my childhood fantasy that our beloved family dog was somehow immortal. I couldn't imagine having to make the decision to walk away from Elsa, just abandon her to die. My pitiful, juvenile version of *Sophie's Choice*.

And that's when I got it. Like really *got it*. People during the Holocaust were forced to make life and death decisions that affected their children, their parents, their sisters and brothers. I couldn't even fathom making such a decision about my dog.

At least for the rest of that day, I put my pubescent pettiness in perspective.

Elsa continued snoring, blissfully unaware.

As an adult, whenever I start feeling sorry for myself, I read a Holocaust memoir. That puts me in my place, and I snap out of my pity party.

When I watch shows like *The Walking Dead* or *The Handmaid's Tale,* (which don't feel so far-fetched in our current state), I think about what I would do in such a world. My pets are always part of my escape plan. If a nuclear bomb explodes when I'm not at home, I would drive home to rescue my beloved dog or cat (once I had located my son and husband and parents). I would share my limited food supply with them and never do what Luke Skywalker did with the tauntaun.

I have accepted that I won't last long.

GOODBYE, ELSA

My first summer home from college stretched on, seemingly everlasting. All I wanted to do was return to school, back to my freedom and fun.

Mom and Dad had given up on Elsa's diet. Dad said, "Food makes her happy." She didn't look like she had gained any significant weight over the semester although her age showed in her slower gait and her baby steps up and down the stairs.

Sister married in August, so most of my summer consisted of working at a retail store and helping Mom with party favors. I grumbled as I sat at the table, my fingers turning green from the floral tape used to transform Hershey Kisses into roses. Mom, frazzled from wedding preparations, smoked as I complained. "Why am I the one making her party favors?"

Mom inhaled her cigarette, then let the smoke out. "It will all be over in a month."

Even though I didn't have a boyfriend, much less a groom, I started envisioning my own wedding—everything pink and Elsa as my flower girl. Mom said, "Churches aren't going to allow a dog."

"I'll have an outdoor wedding then." I didn't want a church wedding anyway, I only wanted the pews and the aisles so I could drape tulle between them, reminiscent of *Steel Magnolias* or the less extravagant *Sixteen Candles*.

Some of our out-of-town relatives stayed at our house, a decision Mom later vowed would not happen when I got married. Elsa had plenty of company, people there to let her in and out during the rehearsal and dinner. By now she was 10 years old, overweight and geriatric, a perfect pet for chaotic times since she was the only calm one in the room.

Before I went back to school, Elsa and I vegged out on the floor. Based on the pictures, we were eating Cheetos Puffs. Someone snapped a picture with a cheesy poof in the air headed straight for Elsa's mouth. In another, I leaned over Elsa's sleeping head, fanning out my blonde hair to look like her wig.

Those would be the last pictures of Elsa.

When I left for college a week later, Elsa didn't have much of an appetite nor much energy. No one was all that alarmed, although I couldn't wait to get back to school and didn't pay much attention to anything else. I kissed Elsa goodbye, told her to feel better, and bounded out the door. If only I had known that was the last hug I would give her.

When I called Mom to lament about the boy I had a crush on who was stupid and flunked out of school, she confessed Elsa had stopped eating. "Oh no," was my weak reply. On Wednesday, Mom left a message on my answering machine. "Elsa gobbled up her Swiss steak and chewed on the bone. She's feeling much better." Mom's elated tone revealed that she had been worried about Elsa's lack of appetite, but I was too selfish to put it all together. I was simultaneously happy and guilty. Happy that Elsa was better, ashamed that I had neglected to call to find out how she was doing. In fact, I hadn't even thought about Elsa's health that week at all.

Our first full weekend at college didn't disappoint. My friend and I giggled at everything, she drank, I danced, and we already had a cache of inside jokes to occupy us for months. Saturday night we stayed out until three in the morning, wondering how we had survived all summer without each other and our little adventures.

My phone rang way too early the next morning. Mom's oddly perky voice greeted me. "Your Dad and I are going to drive down and take you out to breakfast." Mom hung up the phone before I could articulate a cohesive question regarding her strange request. It was an hour's drive, but in those days, it took me at least 90 minutes to ready myself.

I pounded on my friend's door, who lived next to me in the dorm. She stumbled to the door, confused as I was. We both collected our shower gear and dragged our asses to the bathroom.

My parents had never come to visit me at college my freshman year, only when they had to bring me home since they didn't allow me to drive the Thunderbird to college. Why this impromptu trip didn't worry me showed how selfish my world was at the time (or perhaps how exhausted I was from such little sleep). It didn't even occur to me that something was wrong.

I had just blow-dried my hair when my parents arrived. As they sat down in my dorm room, I began curling my hair. Mom asked about our fraternity party with the live band the night before. We chatted and then I asked, "How's Elsa?"

Mom and Dad looked at each other, then Mom said, "She was really sick," as tears filled her eyes. I looked at Dad, silently pleading that he would contradict Mom's statement, yet tears sat in his eyes as well. I had never seen my father cry before, not even when his father died. They didn't have to say anything more. I knew what had happened. Tears gushed from my eyes as the curling iron in my hand began to slip. Mom grabbed the iron before it burned me, and I sat on the floor and cried.

Friday my parents took Elsa to the vet. She had cancer and due to her health and age, would not survive any invasive procedures. They put her to sleep; Mom stayed the whole time, so Elsa wasn't alone. Mom called Sister and told her what had happened. Sister later told me that Mom wanted to wait to tell me, but Dad convinced her otherwise. Mom didn't want to ruin my weekend, so they waited until Sunday to bring me the news.

Although I understood why my parents wanted to tell me in person, I was mad for not knowing. For the last 48 hours I had partied and giggled while my parents had sat with Elsa while she died. Not that I could have done anything about it, but I felt I should have known or they should have told me. I wouldn't have cared to have my weekend ruined. I didn't want my parents making such decisions for me now that I was an adult. But I said nothing, for what could I have said? I would never pet Elsa's thick fur again or sit next to her on the floor and give her a hug.

But maybe I could have said goodbye.

I didn't feel like eating, but my parents insisted we get some brunch. A small college town on a Sunday morning doesn't have much to offer, so we ate at one of the only sit-down restaurants. I picked at my food as my parents attempted small talk. An old couple sitting a few tables away provided our entertainment. Based on the decibel of the old lady's voice, the old man was hard of hearing. They were discussing dialysis of all things. When the old guy declared, "Now that Matlock was a good lawyer," my friend couldn't smother her laughter. Grateful for the distraction, I silently thanked those old people for their presence.

Since Elsa's death, my first few weeks of school had not been all that my friend and I imagined. My new roommate turned out to be a vampire. Our party plans disintegrated with each passing weekend (now that we were no longer Fresh Meat Freshman, party invites were not as abundant for sophomores), and my classes brought me anxiety, although I couldn't figure out why since school rarely caused me stress.

For my creative writing class, I wrote a poem about Elsa. My instructor hated anything sentimental or romantic or nostalgic, so I didn't care much for her, although my B-grade on the poem was rather kind. Perhaps my instructor did have a heart after all.

Because Elsa loved lying underneath the deck in the corner near the gate, Mom and Dad buried her ashes there, with her tags and Aids Monkey to keep her company. College provided a natural separation from Elsa, so I could ignore her absence in my dorm for she was never there to begin with. But at home, I knew the void that awaited me. Before my parents picked me up in November, I had a lunch date with a guy I begrudgingly agreed to see. He gave me a yellow rose. I gave him an eye roll. The flower looked more beautiful—more yellow and happy—on Elsa's grave. I dusted off the small wooden plaque Dad had made and whispered, "I miss you. I'll never forget you."

Mom and I went shopping for a Barbie-sized Christmas tree, which I decorated and set out under the deck after Thanksgiving. Well after Christmas when the roll of film was filled and developed, I saw a photograph of me under the deck. Mom had taken my picture from the basement window as I wished Elsa a Merry Christmas.

Without Elsa to greet me at the steps, the house sat quiet, despite the television that created obnoxious background noise. Watching TV in the living room at night was almost unbearable. My parents' continual snacking without a patient dog waiting for a Cheeto nearly brought me to tears.

Those firsts—the first weekend home, the first Thanksgiving without Elsa sitting in the kitchen waiting for turkey skin, the first Christmas without her opening presents—are always the hardest. As fond as our memories may be, they can never fill the void that a death leaves behind.

Elsa was the first pet I lost where I understood that loss—the painful mortality of my imagined immortal dog. Grumpy Bear didn't talk (I think), and my dog died just like every other dog.

And still, I hadn't gotten to say goodbye.

LOVE & SAVANNAH

My parents never had another pet.

The next fall, the house welcomed the furry pitter patter of paws after my sister and her husband rescued a dog from the pound. They didn't know how old she was, maybe one or two. She looked like a skinny golden retriever, with long legs, a long snout, and floppy ears. Her short golden hair wasn't soft like Elsa's. Mom referred to her as a mutt in the family Christmas letter. Her name was Savannah.

I babied Savannah. I brought her gravy-basted bones since Sister wouldn't allow those in her house because they left smudges on the carpet. Savannah was a quiet dog, yet looked ill at ease most of the time, unsure if her environment was safe or threatening. She would have made the perfect cuddle snuggle dog for her lack of hyperactivity, but I doubt she received any snuggle time or hugs. She was well-behaved, never jumped on furniture, never jumped at all, in fact. The most excitement I saw from her was when Dad took her for walks. That appeared to be her favorite thing to do.

I loved having a dog visit the house again, but it never felt the same. Savannah didn't live there, and she wasn't a part of the household.

When my best friend and I moved out of the dorms the year after Elsa died, I wanted a cat, but she said she was allergic (she didn't like cats). She didn't need a dog since she still had her dog at home. Now that I had officially moved out of the house, I wanted my own furry friend, but it was not to be. I had to make do with my stuffed animals. My friend and I displayed stuffed animals on our beds (one of the many reasons neither of us had boyfriends) and buckled our toddler-sized stuffed animals, The Bunny and Odie, in the backseat during road trips (another of the many reasons neither of us had boyfriends). Our friends who were boys would torture our animals when they came over to our apartment to party. Molly the Cow and Pietro the Pig, our puppet animals, would be thrown or kicked across the room. Sometimes they would body slam Odie or The Bunny. Animals on our beds would fly down the hallway into the living room. We created house rules to follow: if they hit one of our animals, we'd break one of their cigarettes. If they kicked or threw an animal, we'd take their whole pack of cigarettes.

Our rules had little effect.

Tony was one of the boys who always came over to our apartment. We started out as friends. Because he was smart, witty, and appeared to accept my eccentricities, I found him charming and boyfriend potential.

Tony was three years older than me, aloof, and didn't care what others thought. That trait alone clicked between us. He didn't care what was cool, trendy, or what would earn him praise from others. Neither of us compromised our ideals under peer pressure, not caring how we might be perceived by others (although my perfectionism still held me back).

And he made me laugh. My closest girlfriends had always been hilarious, with a sense of humor like a character on *Saturday Night Live*, eccentric or snarky, commenting on others' behavior that brought on a fit of giggles. I adored Tony's comedic observations and deadpan delivery.

After three months of regularly hanging out, he had yet to ask me out, which landed him into the Jim and Pam of will-they-or-won't-they those first couple of seasons on *The Office* (which didn't exist yet, but we certainly weren't like Ross and Rachel). We flirted, but I could never quite grasp if it would turn into something or not.

Boys had long stopped being gross, but sometimes they were frustratingly stupid, while I remained idiotically naïve.

After I turned 21, Tony and I started dating—kind of. He kissed me, I spent the night, then we hung out some more. Nothing official exactly, so Mom took charge. "Invite him to our house."

That was the last thing I wanted to do, but Mom had a point. If he was interested in a serious relationship, he would accept the invitation. No one casually dating would want to spend the weekend with a not-quite-your-girl-friend's family. I asked Tony, "Would you want to come home with me over Memorial Day weekend? It will probably be really boring…"

Without hesitation, "I'd love to."

Mom and Sister cornered me within hours of our arrival, telling me some variation of "He's a keeper."

But it was Savannah who certified it, like she was the notary as I signed the papers.

Tony came from a family who hunted—deer, mostly. After my diatribe on Bambi, Tony vowed he had never shot a deer nor would he ever. He didn't partake in the murderous festivities or had any desire to stalk an animal and shoot it, like the premeditated murder I witnessed so long ago in *Bambi*. Plus, he never uttered such terrifying words as "I hate cats" or "I'm not a cat person" or "Dogs are stupid" or even the horror of "I'm allergic to dogs and/ or cats."

During a lull in our card game, Tony sat on the floor as he chatted with my family. Savannah walked over and sat next to him. Tony petted her as he continued talking. She laid down on her side up against him. Tony didn't move, comfortable with a dog invading his space, Savannah content as someone rubbed her.

Then Tony spoke to Savannah, with a voice a bit higher than normal, "Someone likes their belly rubbed."

I knew at that moment Tony would be my future husband.

HELLO, GINGER

While other children fantasized of adulthoods with money and stardom, I dreamt of little lap dogs, preferably ones I could carry around in a big purse. (I was Elle Woods minus the sorority long before *Legally Blonde* premiered in theaters.) I loved fluffy dogs with curly tails, perhaps to remind me of Elsa. The perfect breed for me: Pomeranian.

I imagined having two: one sable, one white, named Cinnamon and Sugar. They would sleep in little princess beds and follow me around everywhere.

Tony would have preferred a bigger dog, but his indecision couldn't win over my insistence. We searched the pound first, but the only dogs available were big dogs, rottweilers and pit bulls, or just run-of-the-mill labs, dogs that could not be lap dogs, nor appropriate for such names as Cinnamon and Sugar.

Just a couple of weeks after we married (which was all pink with tulle between the pews, but I had to settle for a human flower girl), Tony found Pomeranians for sale.

By the time we met with the breeder, only a hyperactive sable-colored female remained. We met her in a grocery store parking lot. The little dog bounced around, dancing on her hind legs, running around us in circles.

I had to have her.

We paid 350 dollars for her, an outrageous fortune for two newly married college students, neither of whom had full-time jobs. The puppy had papers, which we didn't even want, but hellbent on a puppy and Tony wanting to make me happy, we drove home with a frothing furball. I imagined this was how it felt on *thirtysomething*—even my wedding had been bound by extended families' limits and expectations. But a dog was all *mine*.

Without the Sugar, I couldn't name her Cinnamon because that would just make her sound like a stripper. I settled on a different spice: Ginger. All my dreams came true in that moment, so I assumed it would end happily ever after.

Hours later, Tony and I looked at each other exasperated. What had we done? Neither of us had any experience house-training a puppy and we had no idea that a puppy was more demanding than a newborn baby (which we didn't have experience with either). I dared not utter a word of complaint though, especially to Mom, who was disgruntled that we bought a puppy before we went on our honeymoon, because she would have to dog-sit while we vacationed in Maui.

At night and when we went to work or class, we corralled baby Ginger into our little hallway. Our small box-shaped house had two bedrooms with a short, carpeted hallway linking the rooms together. A baby gate blocked access between the living room and the hallway, and we shut all the doors. Baby Ginger whined and barked most of the night, upset in her isolation. When we returned home, she wiggled ferociously, as if her little body would unhinge from her head. Neither of us complained as we cleaned up accidents and took her out on a leash several times a day.

We were exhausted. We had a little furry baby dependent upon us, yet we could barely take care of ourselves. But within all that responsibility held a perfect joy—Ginger made me so happy. Nothing else mattered. A new light emanated from our house; it held a different energy with the addition of a tiny puppy. No matter how many childhood mementos decorated the rooms—Marilyn Monroe's framed picture on the living room wall or even Grumpy Bear sitting on our office bookshelf— it was Ginger who gave our small, rented house a soul. I felt less burdened even with more responsibility.

In just a couple of weeks, Ginger was sleeping with us at night, and we trusted her enough to let her roam the house while we were gone. We only found the occasional piddle spot when we slept in too long on the weekends.

I cringe at my reckless younger self yet envy her carefree spontaneity. At that age, I didn't debate every decision nor worry about its long-term consequences. We wanted a puppy, so we bought a puppy, despite the cost, the care, the disruption, the responsibility. Our immaturity somehow equated to an endless supply of patience simply because we didn't know any better.

Every time I went to Walmart or Target, I came home with treats or toys for baby Ginger. I would not recommend this as she continued to expect it up until she died that every plastic bag held a surprise for her. Her favorite: Dingos, little rawhide bones with a red chunk twisted into the middle, just her size. She ate two or three a day until we felt the cost in our Cratchit budget, so we cut it back to just one a day.

Coming home became my favorite part of every day. Opening the door and being greeted so excitedly—every single time—lifted my mood, put a smile on my face, and made me feel like I mattered, like someone cared that I had left and now cared that I had returned.

I loved taking Ginger for walks and Tony, a smoker, didn't mind leashing her up every time he smoked. We loved snuggling on the couch with her on our laps. She claimed all blankets as her own, but my sunflower blanket, a high school graduation gift, became her favorite, especially since I used it all the time. Ginger spent her afternoons perched on the back of the couch so she could look out the window. We didn't buy her a bed since she used our bed or the couch or whatever blanket as napping spots.

Despite her hyperactivity, she was an excellent traveler, dancing around every time we said, "You want to go for a ride?" She learned quickly: stay, speak, shake, sit, walk. Her stuffed purple and black ladybug emitted crackling bug noises and became her favorite toy. We'd say, "Go get your bug" and she'd run to find it, bringing the bug back to us.

Ginger declared goulash her favorite meal. How she differentiated between goulash and chili or even lasagna baffled me. She danced around the kitchen as I fried the hamburger (barely a fourth of a pound even though Mom had always used a whole pound) and boiled the macaroni, her little paws skittering around me. She tried to wait patiently as I let it simmer, but soon panted and pawed at the stove as if that would speed the process. I filled a small plate with goulash and told her, "It's hot. We have to let it cool down first." She didn't care how hot it was as she paddled her little front paws toward the countertop. I could barely place the plate on the floor before her nose was on the dish. She ate around the edges of the plate first, leaving a small pile of hamburger in the middle. Only a dog of mine would leave the meat behind. I made goulash every April 26 on Ginger's birthday (with a vanilla cupcake topped with vanilla frosting for dessert).

Ginger went everywhere with us except Hawaii. I brought back a little stuffed squirrel for her. I missed her while we sat on the beach and said how much she would have enjoyed running in the sand and frolicking in the ocean. She always came with us when we spent the weekends with family, and she stayed with us in hotels when we went to Minneapolis. We were poor anyway, so we rarely traveled in those early days, preferring to stay close to home, which now felt complete with Ginger in our family.

Ginger tightened the bond in our marriage as Tony and I struggled with life, responsibility, and each other those first couple years.

THE NEW BABY

Ginger was five years old when I brought baby JJ home from the hospital. I worried Ginger would be forced into the background of life, the older child who's supposedly neglected when the younger one becomes the mythical favorite. I was always a one-egg basket person: one best friend, never a group; a boyfriend that always replaced the one best friend; one passionate hobby that overtook all others; overdoing events like Christmas or birthday parties; going overboard with teaching lessons and activities. I was always thorough, thought of everything, and planned every possible detail. Because such behavior exhausted me, I found little balance in life.

When I was pregnant, I bought a soft little reindeer at Christmas and held it back for Ginger until JJ was born in March. I didn't want her to feel forgotten with the addition of a new baby in the house. I wrapped the reindeer and stuck it in the pocket of my labor bag. That little reindeer was just as important to me as my hot rollers and makeup.

Ginger took advantage of my protruding belly, resting

her head on it like a pillow. While I waited for the dreaded delivery, I continued to operate as though I wasn't pregnant. I contorted myself to paint my toenails while I whispered thanks for having a relatively uneventful pregnancy, which meant I'd pay for it during delivery.

Everything went wrong once my labor began three weeks early. I left Ginger mid-morning on a Thursday. I would not see her again until Friday of the following week.

First, I had an emergency C-section; then baby JJ was whisked away to the NICU (Neonatal Intensive Care Unit), where he stayed for five days. Then baby JJ was moved into a tiny room with me and Tony for another couple days before they discharged him. I refused to set foot in the house without my baby, so I remained at the hospital the entire time (except when I was about to crack and Mom booked me and Tony a hotel room downtown so that we could be together and take a nap and eat, but that's another story).

Because I went into labor about three weeks prematurely, the doggie-sitting plan was also disrupted. The original plan: Ginger would stay at my parents' house until we came home from the hospital. That way, Tony wouldn't have to worry about going back and forth from hospital to home to care for Ginger. On the surface, this could still occur, only for triple the time due to my C-section and JJ's stay in the NICU. But the timing destroyed poor Ginger's sense of security. My sister and her husband had made travel plans, so my parents were already watching Savannah and their three-year-old grandson.

While I was still hooked up to IVs and holding back sobs (afraid of my staples splitting open and having my insides fall out), someone made sure I knew that one of the dogs had peed on the floor overnight and apparently Ginger was to blame. Meanwhile, Mom was frustrated because my sister didn't adjust her plans to accommodate my premature labor and complications from it. Since Mom spent as much time at the hospital as possible, Dad dealt with a three-year-old who pooped his pants. If such stories had been told with the gusto of a *Seinfeld* episode, they would have been laughable, providing a hilarious distraction during my first depressing days as a new mother. Instead, I became a sponge that soaked up everyone else's irritation. I already had enough to panic over that trumped anyone else's minor aggravations—*the health of my infant son*—not to mention my own mental and emotional stability, yet now I worried about Ginger too.

After that first night, I told my exhausted and over-wrought husband, "You go sleep at home. JJ's in the NICU and there's nothing you can do for me here. At least you can take care of Ginger."

I don't know if that made Tony feel better or worse: better because he could get a good night's sleep at home in his own bed or worse because now I put more responsibility on him to take care of the dog. I concluded it was good, as it would allow more time for Tony to smoke.

Worrying about Ginger gave me something I could fix. I couldn't undo my C-section and I couldn't make my baby's lungs breathe on their own. But I could resolve everyone's dog problems, planting it at my husband's feet.

That week was the longest of my life. It should have been one of the happiest, but it was one of the most stressful and saddest weeks I've ever experienced.

After five days in the NICU, the doctors released JJ from intensive care, but not from the hospital. We crammed into a tiny hospital room, with JJ's monitors filling up most of the space. That night, my parents took Ginger back, where she stayed for the next two days until JJ was officially released from the hospital.

When Tony finally locked JJ's car seat in place, that secure click I heard for the first time rescued me from hospital hell. That click would ground me as I heard it hundreds of times over the next few years, a gentle reminder that things could be so much worse. JJ was healthy, needing nothing additional from the hospital despite what doctors had told us in the beginning. Tony carried the car seat into the house while I brought in my bag and the wrapped reindeer.

Mom had already brought Ginger back over to our house and stayed until we arrived. I hadn't seen Ginger for a week. Her butt wiggled so fast it was only a blur as she hopped up and down. She was overstimulated by my appearance and the new bundle in the car seat. The reindeer sat unopened until Ginger had sufficiently sniffed us all.

She danced around baby JJ, unsure if this new thing was staying or going. We had given Mom a blanket that JJ used at the hospital. Mom brought it home for Ginger to smell, so the new baby would appear familiar at first meeting. Ginger kissed JJ's cheek while he sat in his car seat. When Tony held JJ, Ginger smelled JJ's tiny fingers.

Once Ginger's overstimulation subsided, she settled back into her routine. Even though a new baby had usurped her spot as an only child, she still had seniority in her mind. If JJ drifted off to sleep in the corner of the couch with his head on the pillow, Ginger sat above him with a sigh for he had taken her napping place. I had to slide Ginger's fluffy tail from JJ's face, running interference as my two babies napped. If JJ napped on Tony's chest, Ginger settled on his legs. If JJ napped on his blanket on the floor, Ginger perched just on the edge of the blanket, never far from JJ. Tony could hold a growing baby in one arm and Ginger in the other, which I could not. When I tucked JJ securely into his crib, Ginger danced around my feet, knowing that she had me to herself for awhile, the rest of the house baby free.

I never wanted Ginger to feel like she was replaced. Since I had treated Elsa like a sister, it only made sense I would treat Ginger like a daughter.

NO ONE CAN IGNORE A PUPPY

Ginger adapted well to the new intruder in her home. I envied her at times because I experienced moments when I did not.

Routine saved me from insanity, but such rigidity ruined what little laisse-faire attitude I barely possessed Before Baby. I was never one of those people with the life philosophy of "Whatever happens, happens." I liked my world orderly, neat, predictable, and cute. I could not control the day's outcome, baby's mood, or my hormonal surges. (And did I mention erratic unfathomable panic attacks?) I relished the calm days, when everything felt Zen yet purposeful and hoped to capture that in a bottle to snort from on my next the-world-is-falling-off-its-axis day.

Nighttime confused Ginger. At first, she followed me from her slumber into the nursery. Once she realized this was the new norm, she slept through the cries, fast asleep under the covers. Sometimes I would return to bed to find she had claimed my spot with her head on my pillow, eyes shut, tail curled up around her.

Baby JJ's eyes followed Ginger around, as he grunted—his first attempt at barking—and waved his arms as he tried to reach for her. Ginger was always gentle with the new baby, sniffing and sneaking in a few kisses. Ginger consumed her Dingos immediately, so I never worried about forgotten treats and bones that were now choking hazards. I kept my floors clean long before baby anyway.

But just as Ginger grew comfortable with her new brother, he doubled in size and mobility. JJ never crawled, graduating from rolling to walking at only seven months. If he had a couch or the coffee table to assist him, he could move like a ninja.

And JJ remained determined to catch that little dog.

Ginger slept, curled up on the couch. JJ stood at the coffee table, pushing around red and yellow plastic cups. Using the coffee table for support, he side-stepped around the corner, leaned up against the couch, and grabbed a fistful of Ginger's hair.

Ginger yelped, jumped from the couch, ran to the other side of the living room, and stared at me, as if to blame me. After I removed the furball from JJ's fist, telling him not to pull the puppy's hair, I comforted Ginger. (This is how it must feel for parents who have multiple children.)

Ginger never forgot, remaining alert whenever JJ was on his feet. She took to napping on the back of the couch, high enough from the baby monster's reach, or sleeping in the middle of our bed, ensuring her safety.

As JJ grew, he viewed Ginger as a playmate. Outside, they'd play ball together (or some facsimile of such). Ginger would grab the ball, run around with it in her mouth, as JJ tried to catch her, giggling with delight. When she dropped the ball, JJ would grab it, run around with it while Ginger tried to take it back from him.

JJ and Ginger had developed their own special relationship. I spent many mornings, afternoons, and evenings watching them play together. Inevitably, where one of us was, you'd find the other two. Maybe that's why they got along so well. I included both of them in everything we did. If we went to the Renaissance Festival, Ginger came along. (They both favored the goats and chickens.) If we went to the Falls, Ginger came along. If we went to the vet, JJ came along. (I had to leave Ginger at home when we went for ice cream. A toddler and a dog going out for ice cream is a two-person job, something I didn't realize until after spilt ice cream, messy faces and fur, and a sticky car. To compensate Ginger's exclusion, we brought home a small cup of vanilla for her to eat at home.)

When we were told that JJ, just shy of his fourth birthday, fell onto the autism spectrum, we were devastated. And confused.

Our online research led us to many parents who described similar characteristics in their children: unaware of surroundings, lack of eye contact, and complete disinterest in the family pet.

We saw none of those in JJ.

Because JJ was slow to talk, my pediatrician recommended a speech therapist. The speech therapist told us JJ was stimming, meaning he would hold up objects and look at them in certain ways. He did this often around wall corners, reversing direction to inspect the corner. However, he would move on quickly, so we just thought our son had a quirk. I had many as a child and as an adult, so thought little of it.

JJ also preferred to do his own thing as opposed to playing with others and displayed an infinite attention span with toys and activities that he enjoyed. He struggled his first couple of Christmases to partake in the chaos of present opening with extended family, retreating to the quiet of his room as his cousins tore through wrapping paper. Yet so many of the behaviors listed within the autism spectrum didn't describe JJ. Perhaps that's why they call it a spectrum.

As a four-year-old, JJ rolled around on the floor with Ginger, playing tug of war with a large stuffed SpongeBob, giving him plenty of leverage as he tried to win. They'd wrestle with her brown rabbit or gray squirrel as he laughed every time her wet nose met his cheek. JJ would run after her, giggling the whole way down the hall, but preferred when she ran after him. He'd squeak her little rubber ducky or Pocahontas, dashing away from her as she tried to grab her toy back from his superhuman toddler grip. The first time they played such games, I panicked, thinking Ginger would bite JJ or JJ would kick Ginger, but they each knew their own strength, never unleashing their full power, for it was the fun of the play that they both enjoyed.

Everything we read online told the opposite. Children on the spectrum didn't even acknowledge the family dog, had no interest in petting it or playing with it, and ignored it as it barked or behaved with its puppy antics.

JJ looked for Ginger after waking from a nap. He loved when she hung out in his room while he tore apart his boxes of flashcards or played with his toys. He'd stand at the sliding glass door and tattle on her while she barked at the neighbor's kids. If I went downstairs to switch the laundry,

I'd come upstairs to find a four-year-old JJ on his bed, covered with stuffed animals, reading a book, while Ginger sat curled at his feet, blending in with all his plushies.

Early childhood teachers concluded JJ was not yet ready to read (which he could at two years old) or could not understand nonliteral words like *several*. Doctors and educators had already lumped him into categories that didn't always fit his behavior. Despite referring to autism as an umbrella, professionals still couldn't comprehend their own desire to automatically assign him "symptoms" he didn't present. Comparing JJ's toddler and current behavior with Ginger gave us a window into a contradictory world where no one could agree yet everyone assumed.

We held fast to those captured video moments of newborn JJ's eyes following Ginger around and of a two-year-old JJ playing with her. While experts left us feeling deflated and confused, JJ's interactions with Ginger offered us a hope we desperately needed.

LIONS AND TIGERS
AND BEARS, OH MY!

O ther than monkeys, I loved all furry animals as a child. Except lions.

It's not that I didn't like lions, I just had a trepidation about them, although I wouldn't have used such a word.

Mom loved majestic lions and fancied stone statues that sat outside regal houses. I agreed with their majestic qualities, but I never wanted to surround myself with them.

In *Rudolph*, the lion with angel wings, a cape, and a crown should have appealed to my fairy-tale and pageantry ways, but I preferred the pink polka-dotted elephant. (The lion's name is King Moonracer according to Google, a detail I never knew in my 45 years of watching.) Maybe I didn't like the voice of the lion or his bossiness, but there was something off-putting about him.

In *The Wizard of Oz*, Toto was my favorite. But between the Scarecrow, the Tinman, and the Cowardly Lion, one would have thought I favored the lion. I don't know if the makeup and costume of the lion gave me the creeps, but I preferred the Scarecrow (I couldn't stand the lipstick they put on the Tinman).

When I was three, Mom made me a lion costume for Halloween. She sewed all our costumes, except the one year we begged for those store-bought ones with plastic masks. Sister was Wonder Woman, and I was Woody Woodpecker. Otherwise, Mom could whip up Halloween costumes like a pioneer woman whips up biscuits. Sister and I were witches and clowns and angels and cats and devils. And I was the Cowardly Lion who hung onto my tail.

I don't know where the idea originated. Dad was a Detroit Lions fan, so Mom embroidered a number 20 for Billy Sims on the back in blue (it was 1980). The mane on the hood consisted of dark brown yarn with little ears that stuck up through the loops. I mimicked the Cowardly Lion, pulling my tail around front and carrying it, which was fitting, for I had issues with the natural ferociousness of lions in the wild.

I would have my son wear my old costume when he was three. JJ was even more adorable in it, but his lion legs were way too short for his human ones, revealing how short I was at his age (and every age thereafter). Ginger dressed as a Viking—football, not the historical kind—when we Trick-or-Treated, trotting around in her purple jersey.

Because our zoo did not have a lion, I never saw a real one as a child. I don't remember seeing any movies with killer lions in them. Saint Bernards, Great Whites, gorillas didn't worry me despite their horror movie characters. Unpredictable grizzly bears bared their teeth and ran with Freddy Krueger-like paws, yet that didn't stop me from collecting bears, especially polar bears.

Female lions didn't worry me as much as the males, so

maybe the manes bothered me.

And then I figured it out in college, when I saw *The Ghost and the Darkness*.

Based on a true story, two male lions teamed up in Tsavo and hunted humans in 1898, a rarity in the natural world. The only explanation for my irrational fear of lions: I must have been eaten by one in a past life.

I finally saw a real lion at the Omaha zoo when I was 22 years old. Long after we left the African desert, the lion's huffing and roaring echoed through the park, causing the hair on my arms to stand, as my eyes searched for possible hiding places should the lion find a means of escape.

Once the internet became loaded with every fun fact known to man, I researched *The Ghost and the Darkness* and discovered that the real lions didn't have manes. Lions from the African brush rarely keep their manes since the branches scrape off the long hair. Years later, new internet research debunked that theory. The hot temperatures kept male lions maneless until much later in life. Either way, I concluded those lions must not have eaten me.

When my son was seven, we moved to Iowa. He always chose a weekend trip to Chicago for his birthday to plane spot at O'Hare. On one of those trips, we saw the real Tsavo lions at the Field Museum. The lions didn't look quite as demonic as I imagined, nor were they as huge as the movie depicted. They were posed like large dogs hanging out in the backyard: one standing up with a large paw in a trot with the other one lying down, his head on his paw. But I still felt ill at ease standing in front of their case as I forced a half smile when my husband took my picture.

Maybe this was the desensitization that Mom spoke of

so many years ago.

THE REPLACEMENTS

"Get out of the way!"

"You can't have that bone in here!"

"Just put them outside!"

That was the new soundtrack to family gatherings once Sister had her first baby. It remained that way for the next eight years.

Maybe it was stress of having babies, then toddlers, drooling all around the house. Maybe it was all that baby brought with it: huge plastic toys that filled up precious floor space, tipped over sippy cups and trails of Cheerios, diapers and bottles and blankets and pacifiers. Maybe there just wasn't room for puppies anymore.

My sister's son was born four years before my own, so I was clueless, selfish, and naïve when it came to modifying environments for babies. Yet the stark contrast of Ginger's treatment Before Grandkids and After Grandkids killed the spirit animal inside me.

The Christmas my parents became grandparents, my sister lived on the east coast and would not be coming home for the holidays. Mom compensated by spoiling Ginger. She bought a toddler foam Scooby-Doo chair and sat Ginger in it for a picture. As the center of attention, Ginger unwrapped her presents, paraded around her toys, then stuffed herself with Christmas turkey.

Once Sister moved back to the Midwest and rejoined us for family gatherings, Ginger (and Savannah) might as well have yelled, "Marcia, Marcia, Marcia!" They became the Jan Brady of the household, ignored and overshadowed by The New Baby.

Other than barking at people when she was in the backyard, Ginger didn't partake in naughty behavior, although one could interpret her hyperactivity as an inability to follow directions. Her small size allowed me to pick her up and place her where I wanted her anyway. She jumped on furniture, which before grandkids was acceptable. After grandkids, her mere existence was barely tolerable.

I was not prepared for this.

I watched Ginger to the point of exhaustion, intervening so she didn't nip at grabby little baby fingers and tried to keep her from licking food-covered baby faces, although I didn't always get there in time to swoop in and pick her up from the floor.

Savannah was used to it by now; plus, she was the Eeyore to Ginger's Tigger. Savannah knew she was invisible most of the time; Ginger was used to being the center of attention. The constant harping on the dogs' perceived misbehaviors sounded like the grating beep of a car alarm.

I tried to ignore it. When Ginger started getting shoved out of the way—not kindly, but a ferociously irritated way—I just kept her on my lap. If I left the room, upon my return I'd find Ginger staring at me from the other side of the glass door, banished for whatever infraction had occurred in my absence.

The dogs were even excluded from family pictures.

Just two years before we had taken professional family pictures while Sister was pregnant. I wanted the dogs in the picture. No one gave me any hassle.

Now Sister's son was almost two years old. Professional family photos again, but the dogs excluded. "You can bring Ginger if you want, but we're not bringing Savannah." While Sister said this, Mom shook her head. "It'll be easier without the dogs."

Because now we're going to have to deal with a fussy baby, a thought I kept to myself.

Ginger and Savannah were also excluded from family Christmas pictures, whether we took them downstairs in front of the fireplace's hanging stockings or in front of the present-filled tree. Dad said, "Don't push it. We have happy babies." But Ginger was still my baby, even now that I had a human baby.

Before Human Grandbaby, Mom and Dad posed with Ginger and Savannah in front of the tree. We piled everyone into the minivan, dogs included, and drove through the light display at the Falls. Savannah sat on the floor in the middle while Ginger perched on my lap. They were as happy as little kids as they watched the lights twinkle.

But now Human Grandbaby had usurped the dogs' spot for holiday cuteness. The dogs were shoved into the background, like some great aunt's fruit cake no one eats but it sits with the rest of the goodies because no one wants the guilt from throwing it away.

Mealtime reignited my dormant dining anxiety. The grandchildren were not Good Little Eaters; JJ was until he was three and then he became the pickiest of them all. Although the dogs would take their places in the kitchen and receive turkey skin while Dad carved it, they would promptly be brought to the sliding glass door and thrown out when we sat down to eat. With all babies strapped into highchairs or booster seats, I never understood their banishment. Ginger and Savannah could barely see inside because the glass had steamed over, from the boiling potatoes, oven heat, and all the hot heads at the table.

I reverted to my childhood days at Grandma J's, saving turkey on my plate for the dogs who were thrown out of the festivities. "They deserve to have just as much turkey as before," I said to anyone commenting that the dogs were fine and spoiled already anyway. My mumbled, "And it's Christmas," was an ineffective argument.

After a particularly trying get together, I said to Tony, "Maybe we should just leave Ginger home tomorrow. I'm not sure I can bite my tongue one more time."

Tony rolled his eyes.

"It's just stressing me out so much. Ginger's not doing anything wrong, but she's constantly getting yelled at." I shouldn't have let it bother me, but I was like a porcupine, prickly spines out to protect my spongelike nature of soaking up muted levels of hostility, the irritation I sensed whenever Ginger's presence annoyed others.

Tony did what he could, taking the dogs out every time he went outside to smoke. But we left Ginger home once in those early days before JJ was born. The second we returned, Ginger knew exactly where we had been and who we had seen. I'll never forget the look on her face that said *how could you leave me?*

I snuggled her forehead, but she turned away. "You would have been yelled at the entire time."

Her look in return seemed to say, "So what?"

So what it was.

With the introduction of grandbabies—the human kind—a subconscious stress hung over festivities. Not that we didn't have fun. Not that we didn't still play board games or card games (although those waned). Not that I didn't look forward to our get-togethers. But a subtle dread radiated from my gut, like when you travel—no one enjoys the long drive or airports or flying, but you're still excited about the trip, the destination, the adventure. Yet now a stress had bloomed from a once easy-breezy activity. I wanted to blatantly ask, "Why has Christmas become so stressful?" but I never did. Between the drama of deciding dates and holiday dinners and the over-planning, I became an integral player in the behind-the-scenes turmoil, which perhaps explained the subconscious stress, which perhaps explained how the dogs undeservedly received the brunt of silent discontent.

The dogs were no longer the kids of the family. They still received presents (I still bought Savannah exotic gravy-basted bones and Sister bought Ginger costumes and clothes, from princess dresses to flower power sweaters. Ginger would wear these costumes for Halloween when she accompanied JJ Trick-or-Treating). During human present opening, adults shoved the dogs out of the way as they interfered with babies and toddlers opening presents. We tripped over dogs while dodging baby walkers and obnoxious plastic toys. At my sister's house, the dogs were incarcerated behind baby gates. My pissiness resulted from my ability to treat Ginger like the child she always was to me while simultaneously also having a human baby to care for. I had managed the transition without relegating Ginger into the land of After Kids, where nostalgic pets congregate and contemplate their past lives in the land of Before Kids.

Yet "Ginger! Ginger! Ginger!" was all I heard.

Eight years would pass before the dogs were once again included in the family Christmas photo. By then, the two youngest were four years old. We had graduated from the toddler phase, which meant the dogs earned their rightful places back into the festivities, no longer replaced, yet not quite equal.

If anything, the dogs should have always been allowed inside during meals. Ginger and Savannah were the only true Good Little Eaters, yet they weren't allowed at the table.

THERAPEUTIC PUPPY

Without Ginger, I wouldn't have survived Mom's cancer or Tony's gambling addiction.

Shortly after my thirtieth birthday, Mom was diagnosed with lung cancer. Both my parents were chain smokers. Dad had stopped and started again several times, mostly prompted by new office rules prohibiting smoking. Mom smoked all the time at home. When their first grandbaby was born, they both stopped smoking in the house, stashing cigarettes in the garage. Dad had essentially quit by then; Mom still smoked, but much less than she ever had before.

Mom's biological mother died of pancreatic cancer at 47. Mom was only 53 when she developed lung cancer.

While Mom's age and otherwise good health made for a decent prognosis, nothing bats your world off its axis as fast as a cancer diagnosis.

JJ provided a much-needed distraction. He had just turned three. His stubbornness exhausted me at times, but he did not throw the typical toddler temper tantrums. An excellent napper, his one two-hour afternoon nap became my undoing.

I tried to keep myself as busy as possible during those two hours, a precious time I used to celebrate. I could clean the house, write, or just relax. But those two hours became my most dreaded part of the day.

I sat on the kitchen floor and cried.

The kitchen has always been my least favorite room of the house. And, other than the bathrooms and the foyer, it was the only uncarpeted room. Subconsciously, I knew the hard floor meant I could not make myself comfortable. I'd have to get up eventually, unlike sobbing on the couch where one could just lay there for the rest of the day, unmoving and destitute. With my back up against the hard cupboards, I sat crying without a box of tissues nearby.

Ginger found me there and did the only thing she could—sat next to me. Over the next couple of weeks, we spent hours on the kitchen floor together.

Most days, she'd lie up against me so I could rub her belly. Sometimes she'd let out a sigh as if to say, "Can we do this on the couch, or at least the living room floor?" Ginger was not the kind of dog to lay on the cold, hard bathroom floor unless she had just come in from a hundred-degree heat. Most times, she napped like a cat, bathing in the sun that shone through the sliding glass door or curling up on pillows, blankets, and couch cushions. But she sat with me every afternoon, sometimes positioning herself on my lap so she no longer had to deal with the uncomfortable linoleum.

I didn't feel like talking to anyone. Sometimes that only made it worse; other times, when I wanted to talk to someone, no one wanted to talk to me. It was easier to just be with Ginger. I could say whatever I wanted and she would listen without judgment. Or I could say nothing and she asked nothing of me. Instead, she licked the tears from my face as I gave her bearhugs. The comfort was her presence.

Some days we'd sit there for much of JJ's nap. Other days, we'd sit for just a few minutes and then find something better to do. I'd join her outside while she ran around the yard. Other times she'd follow me downstairs and curl up on the spare bed as I worked on projects. If I decided to clean, she'd scamper off to the master bedroom and find herself a more suitable place to nap.

By the time Mom had cancer, Ginger was used to all the crying on the kitchen floor. Tony's gambling addiction started when JJ was about six months old. I had grown accustomed to using JJ's nap time to cry.

After dealing with the continual fallout of financial stress and familial arguments as well as the burden of all household and parenting duties, I now worried about my mother's health. I finally cracked a few months later.

The final trigger: JJ throwing up in the middle of the night. *I can't handle vomit.* It happened over the weekend, when Tony was home from work, although that, too, had become sporadic. Tony's job required him to travel, yet he set his own schedule, a random fucked up schedule that only benefitted him. Sometimes he wouldn't come home when he said; other times he came home early, usually because he gambled away all his available income. By year two of dealing with his recovery and relapses, his family didn't seem all that supportive of my hysterical pleas for help and my own family had grown frustrated because I wasn't doing what they thought I should be doing. I stopped sharing the torrid details, but in vulnerable moments with verbal diarrhea, I still told Mom too much, which would ultimately make matters worse. After seeking out several mental health options, Al-Anon was where all paths led (even though alcohol was not his problem), a program I tried whole-heartedly and optimistically, but after a year I had grown disenchanted with due to its archaic, sexist, one-size-fits-all, and protective-of-the-addict approach.

I had to remain the anchor for all of life's responsibilities while Tony did whatever the hell he wanted, which included vanishing, not answering my calls, and avoiding all that life threw at us—in our case, our son's educational and social needs. I was exhausted, but refused to acknowledge much of it, bulldozing through my day as if "normal" still existed. Mornings—under no exception—meant my customary makeup and hot rollers, for my earth would fall off its axis if I didn't stick to the routine I had started in eighth grade. My house remained clean—cluttered at that point because we had long outgrown our house—with a weekly once-over that included dusting and Windexing. I insisted upon a creative outlet, since I knew that would keep me on the precipice of sanity, so I wrote or scrapbooked or made intricate home movies that looked like themed music videos. I taught two classes a week at a community college, which also kept me mentally stable, giving me a distraction and a purpose. Only at the end of a long, horrible, trying day did I allow myself to check out mentally in front of the TV, imagining myself as a contestant on *Dancing with the Stars* or solving crimes on *CSI* (I screamed at the television when Dr. Drew enabled and coddled his *Celebrity Rehab* patients, so I saved that show for days when I didn't feel as though I'd been beat like a rug on *Little House on the Prairie* then stabbed with a fork like Elaine's date on *Seinfeld* then sent through the woodchipper from *Fargo*). Sure, I spent afternoons crying, but I still looked "normal" and accomplished all tasks under the pretense that said, "I'm fine. Move along. Nothing to see here."

When JJ threw up, I longed for the woodchipper.

Panic attacks ran in my family. Mom suffered from them when I was just a baby, her first one overwhelming her when she was washing dishes. She kept them to herself and figured out how to control them. Perhaps I had been keeping them away for months, even years, but the threat of vomit had added one more layer of paranoia to my already fragile world.

Because JJ was a healthy baby, I didn't have to deal with much other than occasional baby spit up. Ginger didn't puke often, but I could handle her small pile of vomit should it happen. Plus, human vomit was in its own category of horror. While I thanked the heavens for a puke-free parenthood, I was simultaneously cursing my existence. I had enough to deal with and now here was the very unpredictable and highly contagious vomit. (I hadn't thrown up since fifth grade and never wanted to do it again.)

I concluded that since JJ vomited once, this would become a new occurrence in my life. And nothing good happens in the middle of the night, further adding to my paranoia and distress.

Come Monday, Tony left, leaving me amid panic and responsibility. Days I handled as always: routine, chores, teaching, meals, playing, bath time, and the now customary afternoon cry in the kitchen with Ginger. Bedtime destroyed me.

The first time my panic consumed me, I had just put JJ to bed around 7:30. I thought I could handle it, but by 9 o'clock I found myself rocking back and forth on the couch, my hands and legs shaking uncontrollably. I called Mom and she said, "I'm coming over." I felt awful asking her for help even though her chemotherapy and radiation had finished. Initial scans showed that the tumor had shrunk. She had lost all her hair to chemotherapy and had lost some weight. But her attitude hadn't changed—panic attacks would not get the better of us.

I immediately felt better upon her arrival. I immediately felt worse upon her departure.

Mom offered to spend the night, but I knew that couldn't happen. I had to find an independent solution. I couldn't rely on my mother every night just because I had some unfounded panic that JJ would throw up at two in the morning, even though I knew the threat of vomit was not the underlying trigger of my current emotional state.

Life sucked, that was the problem, even though it was the vomit that pushed me over the edge of sanity into a purgatory of insanity. The gambling, the financial problems because of the gambling, trying to deal with an addict (which is impossible), balancing a precarious line of enabling and a contradictory independence (you're not supposed to enable the addict, yet you're expected to take care of *literally* everything and not complain about it), being a new mother, JJ's autism diagnosis, and my own mother's mortality had all packed on the panic train. Vomit just sent that hurtling train off the tracks.

Our small house had a hallway that ended with three doorways in a cul-de-sac style: the bathroom, our bedroom, JJ's bedroom. I always shut JJ's door most of the way, leaving it open a crack, while my door remained open. Always a light sleeper, I had slept with a fan whirring since junior high. Motherhood had activated hypersensitive hearing; even with a fan, I could hear a butterfly sneeze.

Because JJ had gone through a horrible phase when he was two, coming into our bed in the middle of night, I bought a bird nighttime sleep soother that hung on the back of his toddler bed. If he woke in the middle of the night, instead of coming into our bed, he could push the button on his birds. It lit up his room while the birds circled around, playing what would become haunting lullaby music to me. Since he had gotten sick, I unraveled when I heard those birds.

Ginger became my lifesaver during those nights when I laid awake in the grip of a panic attack that felt would never end.

We had a television in our room and our cable provider offered music channels. I would find an Eighties or pop or rock channel and sit in bed, trying to calm myself as I softly sang every single syllable of the song, rocking back and forth to stop the frightening shaking that had taken over my body. At first, Ginger seemed confused by such nighttime activity, her sleepy eyes wanting to close, but she snuggled up against me as I pet her nonstop. Some nights, I would do this for hours, not falling asleep until three in the morning; on nights when I could fall asleep, JJ's birds would wake me at midnight, and I wouldn't fall back to sleep until after four in the morning. Just having Ginger beside me kept the isolation from escalating into helplessness. I could talk to Ginger, even if she couldn't help me should something dreadful happen. Her presence meant I wouldn't have to face the trauma alone.

This continued for weeks. I didn't dare nap while JJ napped, thinking extreme exhaustion could defeat a panic attack. Some nights it did, some nights it didn't.

And then after Tony's next vanishing act (i.e. relapse), I sought out a divorce attorney.

Tony wasn't expecting such a drastic reaction to his pattern of recovery and relapse. Usually, his attitude towards our marriage in the grip of his addiction was lackluster at best, sometimes even stating that divorce was inevitable; then after the high and subsequent crash and burn had passed, life evened out. I decided I could not live the rest of my life in such a manner. Those nighttime panic attacks had given me a stark warning—that could be a regular part of my future if I didn't do something to permanently resolve them.

I couldn't do anything about Mom's cancer. I couldn't do anything about norovirus or foodborne germs or E coli or any number of reasons for vomit. But I could do something about my marriage—end it.

My detail-oriented self asked all the pertinent questions to my lawyer, so I thought. I would seek primary custody of JJ, giving ample visitation to Tony when his work schedule allowed, assuming he displayed enough responsibility to care for his son on a strict schedule. My lawyer even stated the cause of the divorce as willful neglect, not just the standard irreconcilable differences.

I didn't file any paperwork that day. Having such information empowered me. Talking to a lawyer empowered me. Having options empowered me.

The predictable pattern of reconciliation began as it always did: Tony apologetic, remorseful, vague in details, but hey-I'll-be-home-tomorrow, which will fix everything. When I told him that I had talked to an attorney, Tony's anger exploded over the phone. His tone changed from despair to hostile desperation. He knew the courts would never give him even fifty-fifty custody of JJ with his work schedule, so he went for the one thing the courts wouldn't care about.

"I'll take Ginger then. She's my dog, too."

I hadn't asked my lawyer about Ginger, assuming she would live with me forever.

After my phone call with Tony, I sobbed. I could barely breathe. I called Mom and my parents promptly came over to calm me down. (It's these times that I was so thankful for my parents, yet it's these same times that made them hate my husband, deservedly so, placing me in this horrible hell for the rest of my existence.)

Mom said, "He doesn't want Ginger. He knew saying that would get a reaction."

When Tony and I spoke a couple of days later, he apologized for threatening to take Ginger. He said, "I would never do that to you."

He went to rehab over Christmas, the first of three stints. Things got better. But it didn't last long.

Less than six months later, it was Ginger who fell ill. She had no energy and little appetite. She suffered a sneezing fit in the hallway, blowing bloody snot all over the walls and carpet, which had me sobbing while I scrubbed dozens of pink spots clean. Tony wasn't answering his phone, even after I left him a tearful voice message regarding Ginger's health. I had sensed it when he left on Monday that this would be a week of disappearance. I had no idea if he would return on Friday and at that point I didn't care. Ginger was all that mattered at that moment. Mom came over to watch JJ while I took Ginger to the emergency vet clinic since my vet had no available appointments that day.

Before I left, I removed my wedding ring. Despite my tumultuous marriage, I had kept my ring on my finger, thinking that symbol of love would keep us together. I showered and slept with it on; the only time I removed it was when I made cut-out sugar cookies. I left it on my vanity, my finger naked without it.

I hadn't bothered to fix my makeup before I left, entering the exam room with smudged eyeliner and flecks of mascara that had caked into my skin with lashes that had clumped together unevenly. The vet was about my age with a kind face and a compassionate demeanor, a cross between George Clooney and Noah Wyle on *ER*. He assured me that Ginger was fixable. He took his time, gently positioning Ginger so he could listen to her heart and her lungs. His ring finger sat naked. I wished to be married to him—he was so nice to Ginger, so careful, his voice so soothing.

Ginger had a bacterial infection. He said spring allergies can affect pets just like people and gave me medication for her. He told me not to worry if it took a couple of days to see improvements—it was good that Ginger rested anyway. Before I left, he told me to call if I still thought Ginger wasn't getting better and they would run more tests.

The next day, I still hadn't heard from Tony. I called my

lawyer and filed the paperwork.

I feared our toxic household had caused Ginger's illness. She couldn't die on me. She was the one who sat with me on the kitchen floor when I cried while JJ napped. She was the one who laid with me on the couch at night after JJ had gone to bed while I watched *Survivor* and my new favorite show *Fringe* (how I longed to live in a parallel universe). She was the one who kept me company when I felt so alone. In return, she asked for little, only her insies-outsies, wiping her occasional dirty butt, and her daily Dingo. She provided the comic relief when I didn't know I needed it and the solace when I couldn't deal with anything else.

HELLO, KIPPY

A cat. An elusive creature I longed for since I could draw pictures of houses with a kitty sitting in the window. I loved dogs, but kitties amplified the Ooh Factor in me. I had even decided I would feed it Fancy Feast, since those cat commercials appealed to my princess personality.

Tony grew up with cats, both farm cats and house cats. Shortly after we moved in together, he brought his old patchy calico cat named Stinky to live with us. He didn't smell as his name implied. We weren't supposed to have pets in our apartment, but Stinky was only going to live with us for a couple of weeks and then would live with Tony's sister.

Stinky was not the kitty I had dreamed of for 21 years. He laid around and did nothing. Neither naughty nor cuddly, he just existed. We'd find him curled up in the bathroom sink or asleep on top of our couch. I didn't bond with him, so I wasn't sad to see him go, yet my kitty heart remained unfulfilled by such a lackluster experience.

Fast forward nine years or so. Ginger was about eight

years old, an old lady who adapted well with a new baby, and JJ was now just a month shy of turning five. I had dismissed the divorce papers after they sat dormant for almost a year. Things were better, more balanced, no more vanishing acts and no more empty bank accounts. I had no idea if Tony was still gambling while he "worked" all week, but it had so far not led to the hell I had experienced for over two years. I was still a single mother for most of the week, juggling tight finances while teaching as an adjunct at a community college. Mom's cancer had forced me to find a babysitter for the first time since my son was born.

The Crazy Cat Lady inside me had tired of remaining silent and dormant. I was almost 32 years old. How much longer would I have to wait to fulfill my childhood dream of having a cat?

Since a kitty did not crawl out from underneath the tree on Christmas morning, I decided for Valentine's Day I would get Tony a cat. I had no idea if he was getting me something for Valentine's Day or not (about a 50/50 chance), so why not get myself something for Valentine's Day too? With all the shit that my life had become, I thought I could fulfill one dream: a cat.

A cat was my Fuck You to the Universe. By this time, having a second child was not to be. I knew that on a subconscious level after JJ was born. Between my arduous labor and the NICU, having another child terrified me. I had just begun multiple battles with professionals and educators regarding JJ's autism assessment. With Tony's ongoing gambling addiction, I didn't dare have another baby even if I had wanted one.

I didn't care that we probably couldn't afford to allot

expenses to cat food and kitty litter. I didn't care that I would now have even more responsibility at home. I didn't care that a cat would upset any sort of household routine or structure I had established. I also didn't think about what would happen to said cat should we end up divorced. I didn't fucking care. I wanted a cat, so I was getting a fucking cat. And if my husband was never going to get me a cat and put it under the Christmas tree in a hat box with a bow like all those vintage ephemera show, I was going to fucking do it myself.

And that's what I did. I told no one, not even Mom because I knew her practicality would spoil my enthusiasm. No one was going to ruin this for me.

Kitties are sometimes difficult to find at rescue centers. When I took Ginger to the vet, I asked them if they knew of any rescue kittens in need of a home. Fate granted my wish. One of the vets at one of the other branches in town had a whole litter that would be ready for adoption in a couple of weeks. Perfect timing for Valentine's Day.

I didn't trust JJ to keep such a secret from his dad, so I waited until Tony was home to meet up with the vet lady. I drove across town to select a kitty. Following Mom's example so many years ago with Elsa, I sat away from the mewing kittens, white and brown patchy furballs that flopped around the floor. I could have sat there forever, their melodic mews a Zen experience.

I wanted to grab them all and bring them home, but I restrained myself, reminding myself that I was a thirtysomething woman, although I felt the childhood joy I imagined I would have felt surrounded by kittens.

I took off my pink furry winter coat and laid it across

my lap. Some of the kittens waddled up to me, but quickly moved on to other stimulating activities. The biggest kitty in the litter circled me. He was all white with only a light tan patch on his right ear and on his butt that led into his tail. As I leaned forward to pet another furry baby, the king of the litter jumped on my back, snuggled up against my long hair, and laid down. I reached back to pet him, and he leaned over my shoulder and jumped down onto my soft pink coat. After staking out his spot, he snuggled my arm, then curled up and fell asleep.

I told the vet, "I want this one," pointing to the sleeping baby in my lap.

I couldn't take him home for a few more days. I hated to leave him there, worried the vet wouldn't save the right one for me. I drove home, practicing how to act normal for a light enveloped me, as if I had white angel kitties circling my head.

I found a big circular hat box and taped a bow to the top, lining it with velour since our new kitty loved my coat so much. The hat box stayed hidden in the trunk until I could pick up our new kitty.

On the way, I stopped at Walmart and bought kitty supplies: a litter box and litter, little toy mice, and kitty treats. I couldn't contain my squeal when I saw a box of Fancy Feast that came with a small pink heart-shaped bowl. My Crazy Cat Lady was out, never to be silenced again.

My kitty may not have remembered me per say, but he remembered my coat. He snuggled up against my shoulder and rubbed his little head all over my collar. He preferred my coat to the box despite the soft fabric inside; he just wanted me to hold him.

"Your present isn't going to wait," I said as I opened the door. Out popped a little white head even before I set the box on the living room floor. Tony said he figured out his present last week. JJ clapped his hands together as a smile filled his face. Ginger, in her older age, wasn't as hyper as when I brought JJ home from the hospital. In fact, she looked a bit put out, having settled into her own routine, already knowing that this little furball was going to upset her lifestyle.

Since the kitty was Tony's, he named him. "How about Kippy?"

I laughed at our inside joke and agreed.

In college, my roommate and I had giggled over a *Saturday Night Live* sketch featuring the Olympic gymnast, Kerri Strug, on Weekend Update. Chris Kattan played her brother Kippy, who talked just like Kerri but with much more enthusiasm. We told Tony about it, and we all started calling each other Kippy at times when we acted goofy.

Kippy the Cat had such a cute ring to it, it stuck.

Now I had a child, a dog, and a cat. I had no idea if my marriage would last. I had no idea if Mom's cancer would remain in remission. I had no idea if our financial situation would improve. I had no idea what tomorrow held.

Except that tomorrow I would be holding a cat. And a dog. And a toddler. And that was all I needed to know.

THIS CAT'S LIFE

I was unprepared for a cat, assuming cats were similar to dogs, except for litter boxes and climbing abilities. That would be like expecting toddlers to act like teenagers, although teenagers have been known to act like toddlers. Adding a cat to a dog household altered its chemistry and briefly felt like we had brought another baby home from the hospital. The home needed time to transition, to reconfigure routines and expectations, while it added more joy with the addition of a kitten.

What I adored about Kippy:

No potty training. On his own, Kippy used the litter box, which we put in the downstairs bathroom.

A cat's aloof independence. If we went on a weekend trip, we didn't need to find a sitter or a kennel. Kippy as a kitten was intuitive but not sensitive. He might have given me a look that said, "Whatever," if I yelled at him for jumping on the counter. Then he walked off to contemplate life. Or not. He'd return soon, or hours later, as if nothing had happened.

Kippy's desire to crawl all over me. He liked sitting on chests more than laps as a kitten, resting in the crook of our necks. And Kippy followed me everywhere—more than Ginger did. He acted like a little dog, a busybody who wanted to know what I was doing or about to do. I had a little friend who stuck his nose where it wasn't needed (but I loved it).

All the straddling. I would find Kippy straddling the banister, just hanging out. It didn't look the least comfy, yet there he straddled as I worried he'd lose his balance and fall down into the basement. He straddled the back of the couch, the arm of the couch, the deck banister, the back of our office chair, the tub while JJ took a bath. He would straddle anyone's back if we laid on the floor and he could even fall asleep like that.

His tiger-like pant when he played outside in the hot sun. His tongue would remain in his mouth, but his mouth would hang open.

His ninja-like appearance every time I opened a cupboard or a closet door. Kippy would wiggle his way in and plop down on whatever was in there: paper towels, cases of Coke, potato chips, Christmas decorations. He'd bury himself at the bottom of closets and even jump into trunks I was in the process of organizing.

Christmas! Kippy took to Christmas just like Ginger. Ginger loved Christmas presents, turkey, and napping on my tree skirt. Mom found pink sparkly satin with silver accents and lined the back with pink velour. Ginger preferred the softer side, so I always laid it out with the velour facing up, like a fuzzy blanket. And now, so did Kippy. They both scrambled for a spot the second I had the tree up and decorated; they both pouted after I filled it up with presents, leaving no room to nap. Putting beads on the tree became Kippy's favorite holiday activity, causing me more than enough *fucks* to blurt from my mouth. Stringing beads on a rotating tree stand with a cat underfoot was dangerous work. Christmas photographs turned into a version of Where's Ginger or Where's Kippy, trying to find the little dog or white cat in a picture filled with torn wrapping paper and empty boxes (Ginger usually rooted in the tissue paper while Kippy squeezed himself into a box two sizes too small).

Kippy's batting skills with every item that fell on the floor. With seemingly robotic arms, Kippy's tiny paws would bat a candy foil or Dingo with fast precision. Then just as quickly, would bore of it, walking away to find something more interesting. Catnip toys were the only toys that held his attention, but the way his pupils dilated and the unending rolling around the floor in ecstasy caused me to limit his stoner time.

And the purring. How I loved the soft vibrations on my lap as Kippy purred away, as if butterflies were giving me a massage.

What I didn't like about a cat:

Kitty litter trails throughout my house. Worse, I had to vacuum the basement bathroom every couple of days. If I waited even biweekly, I could barely see the linoleum under all the litter.

I don't mind when animals jump on furniture, but they must stay off my counters and tables. I couldn't let cupcakes cool or painting projects dry without Kippy jumping up to investigate. I yelled more than I ever have, "Get down," to which Kippy would stare at me, like a football player when the referee throws a flag as if saying, "Who, me? I didn't do anything." Kippy continued staring at me until I shoved him off the counter.

Those front claws surprised me. I was unprepared to walk into my living room and see a cat dangling from my curtains several feet off the ground. My curtains survived, but not my pink satin comforter.

Oh my god—the cat hair. Kippy slept on every comfy spot on every piece of furniture and on every available blanket in the house. White cat hair on a bright red couch and love-seat appears as if it has a reverse rash. Ginger rarely shed, only leaving the occasional clumpy behind. Now I spent extra time vacuuming the couch, using the hose to scrub out the short white hairs that ground into every available soft surface. We would buy a Jan Brady green tweed-like couch in a half-circle shape with a matching barrel chair. Very retro. The cat hair stuck to that fabric even worse, but at least you couldn't see it when you sat down. (But when you stood up, your ass would be covered with white hair. I cringed anytime anyone wore black. Yikes.) And while the rooting under the blankets brought me giggles, the hair left behind brought me only sneezes.

The escape artist that lives inside every cat. I worried as Kippy walked the perimeter of our chain link fence, afraid he'd leap over it or slither through the gap between the gate and the fence. I didn't let him outside all that often because it felt like I had another toddler to watch.

While I didn't mind Kippy's aloofness, I found his unresponsiveness at times frustrating. Ginger responded to most commands, even if she didn't follow the specific direction. But Kippy would just carry on or walk off, leaving me feeling ignored and a little offended.

And Kippy didn't talk that much. I wanted a chatterbox for a kitty, one who walked around meowing at everything all the time. The few times he did meow, it was the best moment ever.

JJ almost graduated from his toddler days—his fifth birthday was just a couple weeks away when Kippy became his brother. JJ attended preschool two mornings a week and had developed his own independence. He valued his alone time much like all the other members of the household, human and animal.

What JJ loved about Kippy:

Carrying Kippy around the house. Ginger was too unyielding and bulky for JJ to carry. But Kippy's slim cat body JJ carried with ease, although the look on Kippy's face said otherwise.

Kippy curled up against JJ whenever he sat on the couch or his bed. One time, I found them napping under his comforter, conked out from all their running around.

Kippy's antics, from squeezing into boxes to streaking through the house with a large plastic bag caught on his neck (I feared someone had broken into the house with all the ruckus I heard upstairs, and then Kippy came flying down the steps, chased by a Hobby Lobby plastic bag whose handles had gotten caught on his neck when he was nosying around my office).

What JJ didn't like about Kippy:

My lecturing him to keep his room at least somewhat organized so Kippy wouldn't pee on his pile of animals again, especially when JJ's favorite cat puppet still had a faint cat urine smell after I washed it several times. JJ's solution: let Ginger into his room, shutting Kippy out, just so he didn't have to clean his room.

Ginger, now a senior citizen in dog years, approached this New Baby with a bit more trepidation than Baby JJ. She had taken more the role of observer than participator in the past year. She watched, then debated if the activity was worth joining. Spending more time sleeping, she reserved her hyperactive moments for times she felt worthy, like barking nonstop at the brats next door who only came outside to torment her or jumping up and down when I came home with plastic bags, because, yes, she still expected a fun little treat or toy with every bag I brought into the house.

What Ginger tolerated about Kippy:

That Kippy had to stay home while Ginger joined me and JJ on rides and walks. Even though she was still vaguely pissed at me from the previous summers, when JJ rode his tricycle a dozen times a day and I would only take her with me on our morning walk because any subsequent walks she would tire from and then I would have to carry her the rest of the way home and it was just a big mess, she relished her Kippy-free walks.

Halloween. Even though Ginger may have been embarrassed over her princess costume, Jackie Kennedy-like jacket, or her pumpkin costume (which she wore her stem hat off to the side, like a French pumpkin probably would), she participated in Trick-or-Treating while Kippy had to watch from the window.

Opening Christmas presents because Kippy had no interest, so Ginger just opened everything under the tree that looked like a pet gift.

And getting to come into JJ's bedroom while Kippy pawed at the door to gain entry.

What Ginger despised about Kippy:

When I tried to leash-train Kippy. I don't think Ginger ever forgave me that morning when JJ and I went for a walk, and I put Kippy on a leash instead of her. She wouldn't even make eye contact with me for the rest of the day. (She needn't have worried. Kippy rolled around like one of those roly-poly bugs, trying to shirk himself out of the leash. It would be over a decade before I tried that again.)

Kippy's Fancy Feast. Ginger always had a bowl of dry dog food in the kitchen. She ate people food with us and had a large variety of treats throughout the day. But when Kippy arrived, I fed him Fancy Feast in the morning and in the evening. While Ginger didn't bother the dry cat food, the Fancy Feast caused problems. Ginger would dive into Kippy's bowl and gobble up all the Fancy Feast, so she had to exit the building while Kippy ate his breakfast and supper.

Fighting over the warm sunshine that shone through the sliding glass door into the living room. Finding Kippy and Ginger napping side by side always brought a smile to my face but a look of discontent to Ginger's. To reclaim what was rightfully hers, she plopped her butt down precariously close to Kippy's head.

Surprise attacks from blind corners. Kippy sat and waited

for Ginger then lunged, paws outstretched as if wanting to cling to his dog-sister's neck. JJ and I giggled, but Ginger looked at us, not amused.

Tony was rarely home Kippy's first year, yet Kippy declared Tony his favorite.

What Tony loved most about Kippy:

Kippy always wanted to curl himself up on Tony's upper chest, snuggling up against his neck. As a kitten, this worked fine. As Kippy grew, he hung over Tony's neck like a scarf. This happened every time Tony sat down.

What irritated Tony most about Kippy:

See above.

Kippy added a new distraction for me, for all of us, really. Dad wrestled with the cat, making JJ laugh while Kippy wrapped himself around Grandpa's arm, attacking his hand. Kippy's antics brought us more happiness than irritation (maybe Ginger would disagree). Kippy blended into our household smoothly. Maybe most cats do.

What Kippy adored about himself:

His ambivalence to Ginger's seniority.

His kleptomania.

We started losing items. At first, I thought I had finally succumbed to the crazies after barely fending them off the past couple of years. I was painting shadow boxes and had small paint brushes drying next to the sink. Later in the day when I went to put them away, they were gone. I thought I had already put them back and forgot, until I needed a paintbrush again. I couldn't find any of them.

JJ started losing all his little trinkets, those plastic pieces of junk that clutter a kid's room that have little purpose but to hurt feet when stepped on. Bouncy balls, miniature plastic signs, micro cars, and his beloved magnetic letters and numbers went missing. I lectured JJ for not keeping his room organized. Every time I cleaned up and organized his toys, he never put anything back in its place.

And then Ginger acted like she was going through Dingo withdrawal. I'd tell her, "I just gave you one. If you ate it already, you're not getting another one until tomorrow." I swear she would glare at me before walking away.

Later that week when I cleaned, I picked up the rugs in the foyer. Under the front door rug hid a half dozen paintbrushes.

Kippy was a hoarder.

We had moved our red couch and love seat to the basement. Under the couch, I found several Dingos, cars, bouncy balls, magnetic letters and numbers, over five dollars in change, dice, Q-tips, pens, another paint brush, permanent markers, a glue stick, plastic bottle caps, Lip I-Vo, ribbons, loose Skittles, Brach's peppermints still in their wrappers, even a spoon. Stuff was packed under there as if Kippy had specifically placed certain items in specific spots.

Kippy had been busy. Considering most of this stuff

came from upstairs, Kippy would have had to maneuver the item to the carpeted staircase, down the first set of steps to the foyer, then turn the corner, down the next set of steps into the carpeted basement, then paw it under the couch. This would have had to have been done either in the middle of the night or while every human was out of the house. I wonder what Ginger thought as she watched some of this unfold. *They deserve this for bringing a cat home in the first place.*

What Kippy wanted to change about himself:

Absolutely nothing. What wasn't to like about a cat?

RECHARGE YOUR BATTERIES

As an introvert, I find communicating exhausting, especially when it matters. Talking to people who don't listen, who lack compassion, and who minimize that which does not happen to them depletes every ounce of energy I contain. After such a tiring task, my frustration and exasperation drain all my reserves. I never want to talk again. It's like the two times I've thrown up in the past 35 years—I swear never to eat again. I eventually did, obviously, but it took me three days before I ate half of a grilled cheese sandwich.

Talking to people can sometimes have the same lingering effect.

When JJ was in kindergarten, another mom spoke to me about the unfairness in classrooms across America. This mom knew me well enough to know that my son was on an IEP because of his autism and that my husband had a gambling addiction. The subject of her diatribe: how unfair it was in her children's elementary classrooms that other children received extra help—and her children didn't.

I looked at her, silent out of disbelief. I wanted to tell her to go fuck herself, but I figured she wouldn't understand my contempt, since she was either that stupid or that selfish. She kept talking. "Why should other kids get more attention? My kids have to do all the work without any help. They don't get anything more for all their work."

I wanted to stab an ice pick into my eardrum, so I never had to hear such fucking stupidity and selfishness ever again.

My reply: "You should be thankful that your children aren't on IEPs, that they don't need any extra assistance, and that you don't have to fight with the school to make sure your child gets the help they need."

"But I bet most of those kids who are getting all the attention don't even need to be on an IEP in the first place."

Yes, our education system has more problems than Gary Busey. But that's not the issue. She was worried that IEP children were going to have unfair advantage over her down-and-out hardworking children, that special needs children would take away something from her children, who earned it without any help.

I wanted to scream and claw my face, then stick my head in a toilet, only after a street sweeper had run over me several times.

Because even if I'm not talking, I must listen.

My battery hasn't just run out at these times—it's exploded, leaking battery acid that may spark and engulf me in flames. It will take weeks to replace my battery, a battery that takes forever to charge—to replenish it will drain out all other energy: creative, problem-solving, physical, and emotional. And for what? So I can sit through another fucking conversation that leaves me longing for the life of a mime?

And then Kippy jumps on my lap. He makes biscuits, kneading my belly as he softly purrs, his eyes squinched shut as his little paws pat their quiet dance on my abdomen. Once the biscuits are made, he curls up on my lap, his warmth and weight a delight as I pet his soft head, the butterfly massage of his purrs a soothing vibration as he sleeps. He recharges my battery, and I don't even know it.

And not a word is spoken.

GOODBYE, GINGER

The fall of Ginger's eleventh year, the vet told us Ginger had congenital heart disease. She could live for a few more years or just a few more months. Since Ginger had yet to develop any noticeable symptoms, the vet didn't seem concerned but told us not to be surprised should we see Ginger start to slow down.

I ignored all of it. I had to. The last few months had been the worst fucking year ever.

Mom died after a three-year battle with lung cancer. She died at the end of April, just a few days shy of her fifty-seventh birthday. The end came quickly, but we knew it was inevitable when her cancer came back for the third time and the chemotherapy almost killed her. She opted to end all treatment. Just a few weeks after her funeral, the tech company Tony worked for let everyone go. He could only find retail manager work that paid much less than he was used to making. I continued my adjunct teaching at a community college but sought out a part-time English teacher position at a juvenile detention center. I couldn't wait for 2010 to end. Surely 2011 had to be better.

Without my mother, our family gatherings lost most of their holiday cheer. The kids still had fun, but the adults never fully regained what we had lost forever. My own separate holiday was easier to pretend all was fine even if it wasn't. When I picked up Ginger to take our customary family picture in front of the tree, I noticed her swelling. She felt puffy and waddled about as though she had gained ten pounds overnight. I said nothing, hoping that by not speaking of it, the *it* I was avoiding could not come true.

After I took down the Christmas decorations, Ginger could only hobble up and down the steps, panting out of breath when she finally reached the landing. We had to pick her up to join us on the couch. She no longer slept with us at night. She still ate and drank, but not with the fervor of her younger self.

Just after New Year's, she spent the morning lying on one side, whining. Any time she moved to find a more comfortable position, she ended up back on that side. She couldn't nap as her continual whine let us know she was in pain.

I looked at Tony, tears in my eyes, hopeful that she could still be fixed. Tony called the vet, who said, "It is time."

It is time. A phrase we use for a myriad of merry happenings: the bride to walk down the aisle, the pregnant mother to go to the hospital, or fill in the blank with anywhere to go—it's time for bed, to go to school, to go to the movies, to board the plane...

And it also means a time to die.

It is time. That's the euphemism we've decided upon for putting our pets to sleep. That too is a euphemism. We're putting them out of their misery, saving them from more pain and suffering. Yet that too doesn't clearly depict what we're doing. It merely explains why we've decided to kill our pets.

I needed my mother. But that was never to be. I felt odd calling Dad for help, after all he had experienced with Mom. I thought I could survive anything since I had somehow survived watching my mother die of cancer, plus a pet's death could never trump my mother's death. Yet it still hurts. Time is a funny, fickle, fucking joke—it helps heal our wounds, only to slice us open with another knife.

Having not yet adapted to a life without a mother, I was now going to have to live without a dog.

With JJ still on Christmas break, we didn't want to bring him to the vet with us, so we had to divide our grief, which was probably the worst decision we made. Tony had to bring Ginger to the vet by himself while I stayed at home to console a six-year-old who didn't understand what was happening.

I sat on the floor and kissed Ginger goodbye and felt her soft fluffy fur through my fingers one last time. I whispered, "I love you." Later I regretted not clipping some of her hair. I turned to JJ. "Say goodbye to Ginger. She's not feeling well, so Papa has to take her to the vet."

JJ saw the tears in my eyes and immediately tears came to his eyes. "But the vet can make her better."

I shook my head. "No, they can't. She's in a lot of pain and we don't want her to hurt anymore."

Tony had tears in his eyes when he picked up Ginger as gingerly as he could.

As if it made anything better, I told JJ, "Ginger will be

with Grandma now. She'll take care of Ginger."

Mentioning his grandma must have solidified the finality of what was happening. JJ, tears streaming, asked, "Why can't the vet make her better?"

As I tried to explain, he said again, "But the vet can make her better." JJ buried his head in my lap, tears flowing. Tony left. I already felt the emptiness.

JJ and I sat there on the floor together. He softly cried while I swallowed my own sobs. I rubbed his back, scanning the room for Kippy, since we both desperately needed an animal friend. He had vanished, perhaps with a sixth sense of understanding.

JJ finally stood up and walked to his room, gently shutting his door behind him. I followed him. When I peeked my head inside his door, he said, "I'm fine. I just want to play by myself." I nodded and shut the door as he asked.

Tony said little when he came home. His red watery eyes said enough. I didn't ask for details, and he offered none. I called Dad and told him. "I'm so sorry. She was a good little dog."

When Mom died, I could remain the daughter. Although I helped with the execution of the visitation and the funeral (Mom had planned most everything), my role was still daughter. I could cry, isolate myself, and allow Dad to make the difficult decisions. I didn't have to call anybody. Tony took care of those aspects for me. He even broke the news to JJ the next morning while my sister and I gathered at Dad's to begin finalizing the funeral. My in-laws helped with JJ, Ginger, and Kippy so Tony could be there for me. Everyone allowed me to behave however I needed.

But with Ginger, I had to be the adult—the parent.

Tony and I had to make the decision to put her to sleep. I had to explain what was happening to a six-year-old. And it was my household that felt the immediate, permanent emptiness, with no way to escape or ignore it.

The next morning, neither of us had to get out of bed to let Ginger out as our first task. Instead, we laid there, listening to the silence of the house. Kippy sat on the end of our bed, staring at us, wondering why we had not yet served him breakfast.

No more insies-outsies, no more muddy paws and poopy butts, no more grooming trips to Petco where Ginger would return with little bows in her hair. Thankful for the snow, which I normally hate except at Christmastime, I didn't feel the emptiness outside in the yard or the now missing walks. I only needed to shop in the cat aisle, avoiding the Dingos that hung on the endcap. It would be months before I would make goulash again; even then, my eyes watered as I missed the dancing dog below my feet. Even all these years later, I think of Ginger every time I make goulash.

Kippy softened Ginger's absence. We still had the pitter patter of little paws in the house. We still had a furry critter to cuddle with on the couch while we watched TV. We still had to care for a four-legged friend with food, toys, and lots of snuggles. A sliver of emptiness filled with Kippy's antics.

I wondered what Kippy thought of Ginger's absence. He was now alone when JJ went to school, and I taught, and Tony worked. Ginger's toys no longer sat in the corner under our bar-high countertop. Only Kippy's water and food dish sat next to the counter in the kitchen. He had no one to nap with. Did he miss her too?

Ginger was our first baby. Our first joint responsibility. The first member of our family whom we adopted right after we married. So much had changed in those eleven years. And now we continued without a puppy under our feet.

At least this time I got to say goodbye.

WINDOW CATS

One of my favorite stuffed animals, not including Little Animal and Grumpy Bear of course, was Tabby, a little tabby cat on his back that sat angled up in a little wicker basket. The shape of his body allowed me to hold him like a baby. He sits displayed on my old-fashioned bookcase next to the vintage cat bookend I found at a thrift store, who sits next to a small metal cat with glasses who's reading a book. I even bought Tony a painting of a cat lounging on a windowsill, smoking a cigarette, which he liked enough to hang in his office.

I could never get enough of cats.

Christmasy cats make me eternally happy. I squealed when I discovered an animated white cat in a red cloak who sing-meows "Sleigh Ride." I carried him throughout the store as if he were as precious as Shakespeare's scrolls. I wrap presents in paper covered with cats in sweaters and hats. Kippy's first Christmas, Mom bought me a nativity scene of cats, which still makes me giggle every year when I set it up in my office.

Cats fill me with a calming joy that assuages the worst motherfucking days. And I needed a double dose of happiness when life kept delivering shit.

We moved to Iowa the year after Mom died. Tony found a better job, so I relinquished my two part-time teaching positions although I worried about everything: I didn't want to leave my dad (he would move to Iowa the following year), I didn't know if I could trust Tony not to gamble, and I already had everything established—a babysitter, my own paycheck, familiarity.

Kippy hated our move. He complained throughout our four-hour drive with long, drawn-out meows of discontent from his pet carrier. Kippy never went for rides except to the vet. I had no way of calming Kippy; I didn't even know if this move would be good for us as a family.

As I unpacked and rearranged and reorganized all my belongings, I found my old junior high artwork. A colored pencil geometric design of a house that looked similar to my childhood home filled a large sheet of construction paper. I had drawn Elsa in the backyard next to a swimming pool. A cat scratched at the door and two more cats slept in two of the windows. (My teacher wrote *great details* on the back—I had even drawn a bird's nest in the corner of the house under the roof.) Is that the life I had drawn for myself in junior high? Or should I have dreamt of more, like Sylvia Plath or Madonna, to conquer the world? Yet as I watched Kippy jump on one box to another, his own *American Ninja Warrior* obstacle course, maybe this was what day-to-day existence was about—a cat, memories, moving forward, no matter if one was conquering her world or The World.

Kippy had many friends whom we stared at through the glass doors of our new sunroom. Orange Kitty visited on a regular basis for months and then just stopped. (Now I had the chance to call him something interesting like Mercutio or Tybalt—although he acted more like Benvolio—yet named him after a color.) He lived a few blocks over, his blue collar announcing his ownership. He'd wait patiently on our back deck until Kippy arrived at the door. They'd paw each other through the glass, then Kippy announced his territory by fluffing up his tail to five times its natural size (but that only happened after I shared some of Kippy's treats with our orange visitor). One time, we opened the door a crack and the two little paws swatted each other, with neither cat seeing the other as they blindly found each other's paws.

And then there was Pretty Kitty. Pretty Kitty arrived late one winter, huddled by my front door to absorb as much heat as he could from the house. I tried to let him in, but he was too skittish. One of his ears was missing the tip. His long fluffy hair looked well-groomed despite his chipped ear. I awed over his appearance, but Tony said I was exaggerating. The pizza delivery guy agreed with me though, asking about the fluffy cat he had seen scamper off our porch. "That's such a majestic looking cat."

I looked at Tony. *I told you so.*

As Pretty Kitty froze outside, I set a heart-shaped bowl full of Kippy's food and treats next to the front door. Kippy was not impressed, nor did he approve of the sharing of his food. He peered out the window at this elusive creature who was just as scared of Kippy as he was of humans. If Pretty Kitty even saw any of us at the window, he darted away. I continued to fill his dish, then added a bowl of water in the heat of the summer so he wouldn't dehydrate.

My dreams were fulfilled when we lived in Iowa: I pulled out of the driveway one day and saw Kippy perched in our second story bedroom window, standing precariously on the narrow ledge. I wished for him to have wider windowsills, so he could sit comfortably, but he looked happy enough as his head peered down to watch me leave. Then on another day as we backed out of the driveway, Pretty Kitty was sunbathing on the front step of our porch. I had a cat in the window and one on the porch.

My childhood dream had come true.

I'M SORRY, KIPPY

They—whoever *they* are—say moving is more stressful than divorce. I'd agree.

By our fourth year in Iowa, Tony suffered multiple relapses, job losses, and that was after a cushy monthlong stay at a rehab resort in Florida.

The end of our marriage was inevitable. I didn't have any energy left to save it and Tony wanted the easiest possible way to move forward, so that meant he couldn't have a household or a wife since we created too many responsibilities. On JJ's last day of fifth grade, he packed up a few things and left to live with his parents in Minnesota. JJ went with him for the summer, since visiting his grandparents had already been planned. In a matter of two days, that was the end of my life as I had known it.

Fate gave me my old juvenile detention teaching position, full-time. I was moving back to South Dakota, leaving my dad again. Tony had gotten a job working IT at a school in Minnesota. Three hours would separate us. We decided amicably that JJ would stay in Minnesota for that year only. That would give me time to find a permanent home. Then JJ would move in with me. I wasn't thrilled with the arrangement but had little strength to argue. It made more sense for him to stay there—Tony worked at the school and JJ would have grandparents for support when at home. My life steadily declined since Mom died.

I—and it was just me doing it all by myself—sorted through the house, downsizing not by choice but by necessity. I didn't mind being alone. Alone had always been a welcome choice to me in the past. In fact, I loved my alone time, which was rare. When Tony and JJ stayed in Minnesota over July Fourth every summer, I celebrated my solitude by turning on the whirlpool jets in our bathtub, blaring my music, and adoring only having to worry about myself—and Kippy, but he was low maintenance. The only time a pang of sadness settled on my shoulders was when Kippy and I would perch on the edge of that same bathtub, with the blinds open, watching the fireworks in the sky. Kippy stood on the tub, his little paws gripping the window ledge, as I watched the fireworks explode above his fluffy ears, like glitter falling from the sky. Fireworks felt romantic to me, the sparkles interrupting the black sky, illuminating the night for brief seconds. And then darkness returned, permanently.

Kippy and I watched the fireworks together that last year. Had it not been for Kippy, I wouldn't have had any reason to get out of bed. Now I wasn't alone by choice. And alone doesn't adequately describe it—isolated was more accurate. Each day greeted me with dread: the dread of finding boxes (which was surprisingly more difficult than it sounded) and the dread of divvying up my precious stuff into sell, donate and keep piles. I had no emotional strength left to do so, especially when it became a forced necessity, not a downsizing desire. I barely ate, so had little physical energy that packing required. I remained in bed every morning, wishing I hadn't woken up at all. I stared at the vaulted ceiling, the incongruent angles distorting the space between me and the ceiling, blurring as the morning tears collected in the corners of my eyes. I tried to think of alternatives to my existence—surely there was a better way than this, surely there was an ending that would keep me and my son together, surely this couldn't be serious (even *Airplane!* couldn't bring up the corners of my mouth). Every path led to the same dead end, a cul-de-sac of hopelessness. This was my start to every morning. But there sat Kippy, by the door, statuesque, blinking, his eyes telling me to get up, at least just to feed him. I would but had to fight the gravitational pull of the bed as I walked back to the master bathroom, preparing for another day of packing and downsizing and despair.

And then a new problem arose, one I hadn't anticipated: the cat.

I thought it would be easy to find a place to rent. I would only need to rent for nine months or less since I planned to purchase a house before the end of the school year. But when I looked online, only a handful of rental listings existed. I refused to live in an apartment because then I would have to also rent a storage unit for the rest of my stuff, which I couldn't afford. Plus, I didn't think I could survive returning to apartment living at my age. The two townhomes I found to rent stated *No Pets*. I could rent a house, but those demanded outrageous amounts for pet deposits. I couldn't afford to keep Kippy.

Ridiculously, I thought if Tony had the responsibility of Kippy, somehow all of this would stop. He shrugged, like with all the other messy details of our amicable divorce. Kippy could hang out in Minnesota at the lake house in the garage with Squeaky, a stray that his parents treated as their own. The three-stall garage offered much space and even had old furniture stored in it. I grimaced at the thought of Kippy not used to the comforts of home: fuzzy blankets, silk comforters, and fluffy pillows.

But what could I do? I had already given up my son, a decision I regretted and lamented with each passing day. I contemplated running away, like the child who packs up some toys in a small suitcase and walks out the front door without a plan—that kind of running away. The townhouse I rented only had two bedrooms; I had to use the basement to store all my stuff. The small living room barely fit my couch and barrel chair; I shoved an old dropleaf table off to the side of my kitchen, using the dining area to store boxes of kitchen stuff. JJ would have been miserable there having only a cramped bedroom to play. Maybe I should just get rid of all my stuff, start over completely, giving JJ room to play...but how would I part with my mother's stuff? I wasn't ready to do so as I clung to a childhood I desperately wanted to return to, where my primary worries involved spiders, finding a seat on the bus, and a slight chance of losing my eyesight like Mary. I cried. And cried some more. And then cried again. Both before and after I moved. Except after I moved, I was completely and utterly alone.

At first, all went smoothly, or at least as smoothly as it could. JJ adjusted to his new school, liked the chaos of the lake house, and spent about three weekends a month with me. Kippy, although he hated the drive to the lake house, his drawled-out meowing showing his disagreement with all that was happening, had also adjusted well. Tony texted me pictures of Kippy lounging on the patio, stretched out in the sun or napping with Squeaky. He fished on the dock with JJ and Grandma, or at least bothered them while they fished. I sent JJ back with clothes and school supplies and kitty litter and Fancy Feast to assuage for all my sins and failures as a mother—both to my child and cat.

Hating my living environment, my only goal was to keep busy. I dreaded coming home, as my empty town-house would never be my home. My new teaching position kept me busy, and I had foolishly signed up for online graduate English classes contemplating a PhD. As long as I didn't think about what my life had become, I could stave off depression and failure, anxiety and despair.

Our divorce was finalized by Halloween. We filed paperwork online, no lawyers, minimal cost—financially anyway.

When the weather turned cold, the newness of my life expired, with Thanksgiving peering around the corner, a Thanksgiving in which I was thankful for nothing. Kippy updates from Tony left me panicked. Kippy had become the kind of cat who wandered around the lake house—not in the house, but the land around it. "What if he doesn't come back?"

Tony's philosophy: "He'll come back. And if he doesn't, he doesn't."

"What happens when it gets cold?"

"He'll come back."

We never let him outside in Iowa. We didn't have a fenced yard, so he never went outside. The few times I let him out on the deck, he darted away to investigate the world he could only experience from the windows. I feared I would lose him, so he remained a total house cat. And now he was roaming near a lake, in areas with thick trees, gravel roads, and coyotes that could eat him.

Tony didn't care about my panic. No one did.

As the holidays neared, Tony grew tired of driving back and forth or even meeting me halfway and became disgruntled with all his responsibilities. Every chance he reminded me how I didn't have to be a mother during the week. He argued over every little expense. I fired back—for the last eleven years, his disappearances had turned me into a single mother. I had to take care of our son, our dog, our cat, and the house, not to mention deal with the pain of a mother who was dying of cancer. He was the one whose gambling had destroyed us.

This sort of cyclic arguing only worsened my state of mind. Some mornings I woke to disbelief—how had my life led me here? Other mornings I let my oblivion rule, ignoring the ruined state of my existence. The mornings I wanted to drive away from all of it and never return were the worst.

I spent much of my alone time sitting on the couch, crying. I wanted my life back, although that life hadn't been all that great sometimes. I wanted my son back. I wanted my cat back. I wanted Ginger back. I wanted my mom back. I worried that I had ruined my son's life—what did the future hold for him now that his parents were divorced?

After Christmas, I fell apart.

Kippy was found with a huge gaping gouge on the side of his face. Tony didn't think Kippy would survive it or that the wound would even heal. Tony and his mom fixed him up as best they could. I was mortified when he sent me pictures of Kippy's injuries. I begged Tony to take him to a vet, but apparently farm cats aren't treated as such, although Kippy was not a farm cat. Tony kept Kippy locked in his bedroom so he could heal, which didn't make me feel better.

To time my move more smoothly, I hadn't planned on looking for houses until at least February. Since Kippy's injury, I started looking immediately, not caring if I had to pay both a mortgage and rent for a couple of months. Now that I had money that Tony couldn't touch, I was willing to part with all of it if it kept Kippy alive.

In a diabolical twist in my already complicated existence, the housing market was a seller's dream. A house would go on the market in the morning; by afternoon, several offers had already been made, usually over asking price. My selection was limited already anyway: I had to find a house close enough to a middle school so JJ could walk or far enough away that a school bus would take him. Trying to juggle my teaching position with house searching exhausted me, both mentally and physically. Because JDC wasn't a district building, I had to drive to another school five to six times a month for meetings, which meant I'd have a longer commute. My realtor said that I was losing out on houses because of all these after school meetings.

I spent several afternoons crying the second I walked through my crappy townhouse door.

Stress always went to my gut (still does). I stopped eating much and then had a digestive meltdown. After missing

two days of work, I went to the doctor. She said it was probably irritable bowel syndrome and to follow the BRAT diet:
bananas, rice, apples, and toast. Buying a house on my own
felt like too much to handle, especially with a full-time job
that had little compassion for my situation. I suffered from
a panic attack one night around midnight, which was the
first one I ever fainted from. Mom wasn't always right: you
could, in fact, faint from just a panic attack.

I lost eight pounds in a month's time and at that point
in my life, I didn't need to lose any weight. The stress of the
year before had already started me on Karen Carpenter's
path.

I went back to the doctor. This was before they asked
you questions about depression and if you felt safe at home.
The middle-aged PA, who was the only one who had available appointments that day, said to me with her pursed
lips and critical eyes, "There's nothing wrong with you, but
you sound like you want me to find something wrong with
you."

I went to a psychiatrist, who refilled a prescription my
Iowa doctor had given me for Xanax (when I threw up my
last year in Iowa, that was my final undoing). He wanted to
put me on a daily pill, but I refused. I only ever took Xanax
at night, when I had myself so worked up I couldn't sleep.
Since I had no Ginger to comfort me—no one at all, not
even a cat—I took a pill that would calm me enough so I
could at least fall asleep. I used them sparingly because I
didn't like feeling groggy in the morning.

And then Kippy went missing.

Tony flippantly mentioned during a phone call that
no one had seen the cat for a couple of days. Since Kippy

had healed from his wounds, he returned to his farm cat life. While I detected a hint of concern in his voice, he too had given up having any sort of semblance of the life we had before. Kippy was just another casualty of our failed marriage.

"Go look for him!"

"I did. I drove around. He'll come back."

"Not if he's gotten hit by a car or eaten by a coyote."

I wanted to say it, but I didn't: *If Kippy dies, this is your fault.* I couldn't say it because I was just as much to blame. I should have taken Kippy with me, even if that limited my rental choices and meant I couldn't eat for the first couple of months because the pet deposit took everything I had left. I wasn't eating now anyway. I couldn't sleep either, as I worried where Kippy was, praying (which I never do) that he was okay. My worst fear when I was little was that I would have to make a missing pet poster and now I was living that nightmare. That night, I took two Xanax.

I used another sick day because I couldn't find the strength to get out of bed. When I finally did, I just moved myself to the couch, watching *Legends of the Fall*, wondering for the thousandth time why Susannah couldn't love Alfred and dump selfish Tristan. It was easier to assess fictional characters' problems than my own. I felt like Humpty Dumpty: I had to put myself back together again for all the king's horses and all the king's men had bailed on me.

I spent most of the night crying. Kippy was still missing, I had to go to work in the morning, and it was now bedtime, and I was a hysterical mess. I couldn't take another Xanax. I knew if I relied too heavily on a pill to put me back together again, I would render myself incapable of doing anything without that pill.

I couldn't breathe as the panic escalated while the clock ticked closer to midnight. I wanted desperately to turn back time, to redo everything from the past fifteen years. I worried I wouldn't make it through the night. Yet if I did survive to morning, I'd only have to go through it all again the following night. And the night after that. And the night after that. Survival didn't mean I had won anything at all.

I dragged myself out of bed with a mission: I dug through totes and boxes, hoping to find a notebook or journal easily accessible. When I couldn't find one without having to move boxes around, I looked in JJ's room. He had an old wide-ruled notebook tossed into a box full of random stuff. I grabbed my pink pen, laid down on my stomach in bed, and furiously wrote. And wrote. I wrote until almost three AM. Mostly gibberish, a serial-killer-like manifesto that unleashed my fury, my frustration, my fear. But that wore me out, as if I had detoxified my mind and put all the poison on the page.

I slept for less than three hours before the alarm woke me, but at least I had survived the night. I threw away the barely legible scribbles, shoving them deep into the garbage can.

I struggled at work, I had to force myself to eat, I panicked at the onset of dusk. Yet all I wanted to do was sleep, but climbing into bed meant the dormant anxiety could come out and play. I read *The Zookeeper's Wife* (long before there was a movie) in the hopes of smacking me out of doldrums that threatened to take up residence with me forever. The Holocaust and animals, a deadly reading combination for me. I cried through most of the book, tears that were not about me. I spent the rest of my time looking for a house.

That was my life for another week.

Then Tony called me. "We found Kippy!" His elated voice revealed that he too was just as relieved as I was. Kippy was found in a neighbor's barn. Considering there were no close neighbors, we wondered how Kippy had ended up there. Maybe he rode underneath a car and couldn't find his way home. He was a bit skinny, but no visible scars although I figured he had plenty of emotional ones.

I had to find a house and fast.

Tony told me he snuck Kippy into bed with him at night. Hoping that Kippy was like my stuffed animals and I could communicate with him telepathically, I thought *hang on just a little bit longer. Then you can be a spoiled house cat again.* My mood brightened when I found a ranch style house just a minute away from my work and from a middle school. The finished basement had a bedroom and a bathroom, perfect for JJ. The house, much smaller than the one in Iowa, still had enough space for my curio cabinet and bookshelves, even though I would have to get rid of even more stuff. I didn't care about my stuff anymore. I just wanted my son and my cat all together again under the same roof—*my* roof.

Tony brought me Kippy before my furniture was in the house, before I could paint, before I could even clean. Kippy was the first thing brought home. I picked Kippy up out of the car and snuggled with him. I was afraid he had forgotten me, but he seemed relieved to see me, although he might have just been happy to be a house cat again.

I half expected Kippy to carry a kitty cat briefcase into

the house, whip out a legal pad and pen, pour a shot of whiskey and light a cigarette, while he sat at the table with his legs crossed, outlining his expectations, safeguarding himself from ever becoming a farm cat again. If I reneged on his contract, he could suffocate me while I slept, like that cat in *Cat's Eye*. Instead, he meowed, rubbing his greasy head up against every corner. He stood on his hind legs to peer out my picturesque dining room window, looked at me, and meowed. I didn't know if that meant he approved or he was telling me of his outdoor adventures and of his near-death experience and never wanted to go outside again. I plucked him from the window and hugged him tight.

Because I was concerned with fleas and ticks and any other injury Kippy incurred over his nine-month long travesty, I made Tony take him to the vet. Tony argued with me, but I unleashed my fury upon him. The vet gave Kippy a clean bill of health.

JJ moved his stuff downstairs, Kippy's litter box went into the laundry room in the basement, and we were all back together again, at least the three of us. Kippy loved my new pink couch. I apologized for the loss of his beloved sunroom and his scratching post, but he liked the big windows in my living room and dining room. He sat on the wide ledge of my living room windows, watching the world outside, probably thankful he was no longer a part of the wild. He would wait for me sometimes in the window, tail up, the end curled as though my childhood self had drawn him there.

JJ acclimated to his new space, playing video games, drinking a cherry Icee, and spreading out his airplanes all over the basement, the space entirely his to do with what he wanted. I sat upstairs on my new pink couch watching *So You Think You Can Dance*, a gray fluffy blanket over my legs, and Kippy curled up on my lap, purring away.

He was as happy as I was.

WHO NEEDS A VEST?

Jonesy, the cat in *Alien*, started it all—my acute awareness of the location of my furry friends in cases of emergencies and disasters.

Other than our one year in Utah, we lived in the heart of the Midwest, on the edge of what was once Tornado Alley. Severe storms were my equivalent to an alien on a spaceship. When a special weather report interrupted *Family Ties*, you headed to the basement, or under a work bench if you lived in Iowa. (Nowadays, weather bulletins turn into special news reports, with overcaffeinated weathermen clogging up the airways with the same information on repeat, zooming in and out of high-powered radars that look like the end of the world is near. Severe thunderstorm warnings are issued with gusty winds and pea-sized hail. When a tornado touches down, no one blows the sirens. It's difficult to know when to take forecasts and warnings seriously.)

One petless year as a child, I threw all my stuffed animals downstairs, one by one, when they issued a tornado watch

223

one summer afternoon—just in case. (And because I always had to worry about something and prevent the worst-case scenario from happening.)

I grew up in a household that watched the weather and believed in forecasts. Mom kept the TV on the newly invented Weather Channel, with its blue screen and flashing numbers. Before the internet, Locals on the Eights provided weather watchers with an up-to-date forecast rather than wait for the nightly news. We were one of those unfortunate families that planned our lives around the weather.

In our ranch house with the full basement, Mom had me and Sister sleep downstairs if the forecast called for any chance of severe weather overnight. While on the surface it appeared fun to have an impromptu sleepover on the pull-out sofa in the basement, Sister and I did not sleep well together. She kicked and I clawed. Because Elsa slept in the garage those first couple years, Sister and I debated about sneaking her inside after Mom and Dad went to bed. On one tornado watch night, Mom let Elsa sleep with us downstairs. We let her sleep on the bed. Sister and I didn't kick and scratch each other that night, but none of us slept that much either.

Once we moved to our split-foyer home and Elsa slept inside at night, it was easy to bring her to the basement. She liked to sleep in two areas at bedtime: either in the foyer or under the pool table in the basement. Elsa was never squirrely, staying by us if we called her downstairs, just hanging out until the storm ended.

And then Elsa aged.

Storms never bothered her before. But the last couple years of her life, thunderstorms triggered every synapse in her brain, alerting her to impending danger. She became inconsolable.

Elsa's last summer, we cringed when the sky darkened. Even before we saw the lightning and heard the thunder, Elsa panted and paced, acting as though she had lost most of her brain and the reasoning to go with it. She whined and tried to jump on furniture at the first bolt of lightning. I slept with my door shut, but she demanded to come in, scratching at it, something she had never done before. I let her in only to have her pace around my bed, trying to jump on it. Using my vanity bench, I helped her step up onto my twin bed. Elsa seemed more comforted by my company as she finally laid still on her side although her panting continued. I barely had room to lay on my side next to her as her girth hogged the bed. Neither of us slept that night.

Mom theorized that as animals aged, their hearing became more sensitive or off-kilter. That was as good as any explanation. Yet retailers wouldn't capitalize on such pet anxieties until 2001 with thunder shirts or anxiety wraps or thunder vests.

Like Elsa, storms didn't bother Ginger until she aged. Ginger's hysteria was more subtle—she disappeared under beds whenever it stormed. Trying to coax her out with a Dingo failed, as she stayed securely positioned under our bed. I'd eventually have to grab her front paws and pull her out, which usually resulted in a yip. If severe storms were forming and looked like they were headed our way, I'd put her in the basement in the spare bedroom to avoid any under-the-bed drama.

Kippy proved problematic during thunderstorms. In his early years, his nonchalance during tornadoes frustrated me. I understood now how Ripley could lose a cat.

Because Kippy was much more difficult to corral, I threw him in the bathroom or spare bedroom with Ginger. Once we moved to our two-story house in Iowa, Kippy lounged on his scratching post in the sunroom, the worst room during a tornado, with its three walls of windows.

By this time, JJ was eight years old, a wild weather watcher. He loved the drama, but worried over power outages, yet spoke as though it would be cool to have a natural disaster occur in our backyard. His iPad became his third arm as he ran around the house with the most updated radar, keeping me abreast of the situation.

Way too often in Iowa, I would stand out on our wraparound porch and watch the sky turn an eerie green. Swirling clouds formed an eye over my head long before JJ's radars picked up the rotation. The first time it happened, my ears popped with pressure when I walked down the hallway. I yelled at JJ, "Get downstairs," and I ran back to the sunroom and grabbed lounging Kippy from the top of his post.

During one storm, I couldn't find the cat. Upstairs during a severe thunderstorm warning felt like the house would separate in two, like a yolk from the white as the wind rattled not just the roof but the walls too. Kippy curled up on our bed pillows, slept soundly through the hail that hammered the roof. But the bigger problem: JJ always wanted to follow me and not stay in our unfinished basement by himself for fear we'd lose power and then he'd be in the dark all alone.

I devised a plan for the frequent severe storms that pummeled us every spring. Step one: Find Kippy. Step two:

Put Kippy in basement and shut the door and make sure it latches (he had learned if he pushed on it hard enough with his paws, it would open and we would find the door ajar and have to search the house for the cat at the peak of the storm). Step three: Stop JJ from running up and down the steps because the cat will get out again. Step four: Give up and just sit in the basement where both child and cat are safe.

When JJ was eight or nine years old, I made the mistake of putting him in charge of the cat. As the storm approached, I told him, "Throw the cat downstairs."

Moments later, I heard a clunk and a surprised meow. I ran to the basement door. "What happened?"

JJ said, "I threw the cat downstairs."

I forgot how literal he was. Once the storm ended, I explained to JJ the difference between literal and figurative language. "Oh, like when you say it's raining cats and dogs but it's not really raining cats and dogs?" I nodded, deciding against telling him how cats and dogs slid off mud roofs during Shakespeare's time, when the phrase originated.

By the time Kippy was in his senior years, I lived back in South Dakota. Kippy would have his own version of panic during thunderstorms: Low and Slow. Before we saw a bolt of lightning or heard a rumble of thunder, Kippy would jump to the ground, glide soundlessly across the floor with long steps, his belly almost touching the floor, Low and Slow straight for the stairs. He had found a spot all the way behind the furnace that sheltered him from all flashes of light and the subsequent booms of thunder. Once I discovered his spot, I no longer had to worry about his whereabouts during storms. He took care of himself.

Julie Ann

After a flooded basement, a derecho, and three torna-does touching down within a couple blocks of our house, I was the one in need of a thunder vest.

FEED THE BABIES

One of my favorite rooms of my house isn't inside—
it's outside, on my deck, in full sun, two fountains
babbling water like a forest stream, pink and red and yellow
and purple dahlias and petunias and daisies, while the birds
chirp and dance in the birdbath and the squirrels crunch on
their peanuts as they perch in my tree.

I bought my ranch-style house partly because of the
backyard. Despite all the old trees surrounding my fence,
the deck provided full sun until evening, giving me plenty
of reading/tanning afternoons. In the middle of my yard,
a Halloweenish tree grew. Another tree grew up from the
middle, so part of it is dead while the other part thrives with
tiny green leaves. My huge deck shelters the bunnies who
inhabit my yard. My backyard might as well have a sign
posted that says *All Critters Welcome*.

My return to South Dakota started my own addiction:
feeding the squirrels.

Now that I was divorced and had my own money, I
no longer worried about gambling debt. I could do with it

what I wanted. I invested some in overly priced critter food.

It all started with the exotic black squirrels when I rented a townhouse while I found a house to buy.

I had never seen black squirrels in person. Black squirrels are common on the east side of town, whereas only the red/brown squirrels are on the west side. (I hope it's not some form of squirrel segregation.) I placed a bowl of peanuts on my balcony and within a day, I had a little black squirrel eating right outside my sliding glass door. JJ created a Squirrel Diner sign and taped it on the door: *Free food, open 24 hours.*

Feed them and they will come.

At my new house, I set a dangling tray feeder from a branch of my Halloween tree. Two more round trays attached on the balcony of my deck. My huge deck spans the length of two-thirds of my house; half of it with a railing with the other half open with just one step down into the yard. My dining room windows are original, filling up the entire wall with nine separate panes (I should replace them because they frost over every winter, but I keep them for their vintage aura). Squirrels dined right outside my window.

I fed them every day, filling the tree feeder with sunflower seeds. On the deck, squirrels feasted on expensive no-shell food so no pile of sunflower shells would form. When I found holiday nuts around Christmas time, I filled my cart with bags of pecans, walnuts, and hazelnuts. My squirrels loved burying those all over my yard or filling their cheeks and taking them home with them.

When I tanned, I put a pile of peanuts on the deck next to my chair, hoping to feed a squirrel by hand. After doing a dance with backward bounces and forward hops, a squirrel would eventually scurry up to the peanuts, sometimes eating one under my chaise. The sound of their little feet on the deck as I tanned with my eyes shut announced that one was in petting distance. Their subsequent shell chewing louder than expected, with their crunch, crunch, crunch blocking out mowers and chainsaws and cars.

I thought my squirrels would be more of the *Sleeping Beauty* variety, but apparently they are not familiar with the story.

They pooped on the railing. They gnawed on the cable wire that came into the house. They chewed holes through my white wicker rockers. They dug up my potted flowers as they played in the dirt, burying their peanuts next to my dahlias. They, along with the bunnies, chewed off my tulip buds and roses. I tried to train them like dogs, pounding on the windows and yelling, "Stop that. Don't be naughty." That did little to deter their delinquent behavior.

When my ex-husband moved back in (I'll save that story for another time as it does not involve any animals), I called him Mr. McGregor from *The Tales of Peter Rabbit* when he threatened the babies that messed with the property. He landscaped the yard, adding pavers and mulch, planting tulips and cutting down weed trees, eventually replacing my chain-link fence with a white panel one.

I had to admit that it was not good to have the squirrel feeders so close to the house. We placed three feeders in the tree. Squirrels still found good burying spots in my flowers but stopped chewing through my furniture. We eat outside every meal during the spring and summer, sitting beneath a fringy lavender umbrella that could have been stolen from the set of *Gone with the Wind.*

Bunnies bounced through my yard every season, making nests in the sunflower seed shell pile that grew each year under my tree. When Tony mowed over a nest one spring, I spent my lunches and evenings doing a head count until momma bunny returned. Many of those babies would grow up in my backyard, finding a warm sheltered home under my deck.

Baby birds struggled to fly over our privacy fence. One little black bird hopped along our back patio. After watching him unsuccessfully jump and flop, I brought out a yard stick, thinking he could hop up onto that, then be close enough to the tree branch. He started screaming for his mother; several black birds swooped over my head. I yelled, "I'm a friend, not a foe," but they called for more reinforcements. Afraid they would peck out my eyes as if I had entered *The Birds,* I went inside. Hours later, the baby hopped up on my butterfly bench, then just flew away.

With a privacy fence, it was safe to let Kippy run around in the backyard. I grounded him several times though for chasing bunnies under the deck and for climbing the tree after squirrels.

I fed the squirrels daily but hated tromping through the snow in freezing wind chills, so Tony fed them for me. I asked him, "Did you feed the babies?"

He replied, "I fed your squirrels."

At one point, I counted 16 squirrels in my backyard at the same time.

Even though I had plenty of shaded areas in my yard, I worried about those babies when a hawk would frequent the neighborhood. A hawk's wingspan in the sun cast a pterodactyl-sized shadow overhead. Even the flapping of the wings sounded like a fallen angel plummeting from the heavens. If the hawk landed on my fence, which was his favorite perching spot, I'd run out my backdoor, grab a rock from the landscaping around my deck, and hurl it in his direction. It never landed anywhere near him for I proudly throw like a girl, so I would follow that up with shrieking and flapping my arms around to scare him. My actions must have startled him enough because eventually I could just pound on the windowpane and that would send the baby-eater back into flight, probably over another yard a couple blocks away to eat somebody else's baby.

I feed the babies on vacation too, an activity that usually makes it into my top five moments of the trip. At a restaurant on Hollywood Beach in Florida, we sat in the open area, eating French fries. Pigeons and black birds hung out, pecking at the floor, gobbling up crumbs and food bits. I fed them my French fries, breaking off a chunk and then "accidentally" dropping it near my chair. Birds can run fast, their little stick legs going back and forth like a cartoon character. Animals look so happy when they're eating.

Even though Tony complained about feeding the babies, he enjoyed watching all the critters in the yard as much as Kippy and I did: blue jays, cardinals, doves, woodpeckers, squirrels, and bunnies turn my backyard into a page out of *Sleeping Beauty*, only without the birds holding ribbons and strings of pearls in their beaks.

THE BUNNY BASKET

My personality oozes from me like the molten part of chocolate lava cake. This is one of the positive side effects of not caring what other people think of me, of not paying attention to what is in and what is out, of embracing what makes me happy—even if those around me think ill of me. My office at work is pink—the same hot pink office chair I have at home is the same one I use at work (why else would T.J. Maxx have two chairs and one still there when I went back weeks later?). As I dot my world with reading cats and autumn squirrels, I cannot help but bring them into the classroom, where I spend the bulk of my day nine months a year (but to everyone's relief, I keep my collector Barbies at home).

It started benignly enough: a pink Easter basket. I needed a place to house candy bars for students who completed a class. When I pulled out my bunnies and chicks and lambs for Easter, I found JJ's blue bunny with embroidered eyes and nose, safe for babies. He only loved it one year, but enough so that the neck wobbled from too many hugs. I performed surgery, sewing small white stitches to stabilize it. When JJ no longer cared about the bunny, I threw him into my Easter decoration tote, always finding a spot for him to sit for a month out of the year.

I brought the bunny to school and sat him in the candy bar basket. He has yet to return home.

The candy bar container is now called The Bunny Basket, and students refer to it as such.

But it's not the candy that draws the attention. Students, most of them male, ask unabashedly, "Can I take The Bunny instead of a candy bar?"

At JDC, teenage boys are desperate for comfort.

They've made necklaces out of toilet paper or hats out of scratch paper for The Bunny. The Bunny has become our school mascot, a lamb maybe the only more innocent animal than a bunny. A paradox for students who are charged with crimes, some violent, some even murder.

That's the power of animals, stuffed or real. Comfort. Peace. Our inner child blossoms in the vicinity of such creatures, no matter how old or tattered our edges.

Animals have the power to heal. This is undisputed. Children—some as young as ten—at JDC need more healing than my classroom could ever provide. An animal would give one more hope, a bright light in a dreary place, something to care for, something to bring smiles and comfort.

Since a real animal will never be allowed (due to allergies I'm told), I've redecorated with smiling animal canvases that intermingle with Shakespeare and Poe and Dickinson. Paintings of animals reading hang above Langston Hughes, Maya Angelou, and Sylvia Plath. A desert tree capturing pinks, reds, and oranges of the sunset acts as a better window to the outside; the grated barred classroom windows offer little view but of a trunk of a large tree and the boys' wing, allowing us to see the rain and snow, but little else. A tropical beach covers my back bulletin board, a permanent reminder of summer during our never-ending winters.

A toddler-sized Piglet waves from my office, left there when we did Pooh-isms, not unlike Ben Franklin's aphorisms or Mark Twain's witty one-liners. (And Twain's Cat in a Ruff picture sits on my teacher desk because who wouldn't want a cat dressed like Shakespeare?)

Animals, fake just as much as real, provide much-needed natural light to an ominous workplace. My only option is to bring nature into the classroom, since students receive no outdoor time. Fake flowers bloom all year. Stuffed animals' embroidered smiles and delightful eyes are better than nothing at all.

THE HORROR
AROUND THE CORNER

O n the kitchen rug. Under the bed. Beside the washer. At the bottom of the stairs. On the plush living room rug. And always when you've just sat down to eat, or have just returned home after a horrendous day at work, or when you're running late for an appointment.

Cat vomit is one of the only things that triggers my hulk-like rage.

I possess an alarming amount of patience for someone who suffers from panic and irrational fears. While I swear like a sailor over people's stupidity, making my son and husband laugh when I unleash a thousand *fucks* over a workplace incident or a shopping misadventure as I re-enact the scene with my foul-mouthed commentary, I never experience road rage, I rarely get impatient at long checkout lines or drive-thrus, and age has bestowed an equanimity over me unbeknownst to my younger self. Yet I lose all sense of peace and tranquility in the presence of cat vomit.

It's not like the dragon lady my family accuses me of becoming when I'm cleaning the house, scrubbing the vacuum hose up and down the couch cushions trying to suck up every wayward strand of white cat hair. It's not even the Griswalda from the Geico commercial at Halloween, which Tony affectionately calls me when I'm cooking supper in the kitchen. It's more like *The Exorcist*, with my eyes ablaze, my head turning all the way around, and my supernatural strength. I'm terrifying, and whatever you do, don't make eye contact with me.

I am ashamed and embarrassed of my response when the cat puked on the bed. My son witnessed my abhorrent behavior.

But I can explain myself. You know how many times the cat has puked over the years? I couldn't begin to count. When Ginger was still alive, Kippy rarely puked. Once I moved back to South Dakota, he puked often, sometimes as a result of bingeing and purging, other times we took him to the vet for expensive tests that revealed no certain cause. (I secretly wondered if this was my punishment for abandoning him for nine months.) Unless it's a hairball, every pile of puke looks like it came from Mars, with its bright brown hue that stains worse than red velvet cake batter. It reminds me of one of my least favorite crayon colors—burnt sienna. The only colors I hated more were raw sienna and sepia. It must have been related to some former torture in a past life, for my unfounded distaste for burnt sienna at four years old left that crayon in pristine condition, while the rest of the crayons were sharpened down into nubs. A premonition to the cat vomit that lurked in my future.

Those climatic moments during *This Is Us*, ruined by the gurgle of an upset cat belly, like the sound of an alien about to pop from a human's stomach. The worst sound in the world is that second just before the cat pukes, when the quiet house shudders with that prehistoric slosh from the bowels of hell, then the slap of vomit onto the hardwood floor. At least you hope it's the hardwood floor and not the carpet. Everyone wants to yell "Not it!" as the designated cleaner, but someone must cave. I prefer dried cat vomit although it requires a bit of scrubbing. Cleaning up still-warm cat puke turns my own stomach. Clorox wipes and carpet spray would be deducted from Kippy's allowance if he earned one.

But it gets worse. Much, much worse. I used to lay out my clothes for the week across my trunk at the foot of my bed. That way, I'd only have to iron once a week. One day, my long black and off-white striped dress (JJ called it my Monopoly get-out-of-jail-free card dress) stretched out across my padded trunk. Upon our return from school, I walked into the bedroom to see two piles of that burnt sienna puke splattered across the dress, with even more puke spatter near the hem that dangled over the side of the trunk.

There's this sinking sensation that starts from my throat that plummets to my stomach then passes to my legs, weakening them with a sudden rush of disgust mixed with it's-the-end-of-the-world-now-that-the-cat-has-puked. And on my dress. Right after work. I'm starving by four o'clock; I don't eat much for lunch on workdays. Low blood sugar, self-created stress, and the wrecked anticipation of putting my feet up for the evening now that I must deal with *this* annihilated any hope for a peaceful night.

JJ never follows me into my bedroom, but he stepped into the doorway after hearing whatever foul four-letter word exploded from my Exorcist transformation. He spoke wisely for a ninth grader. "You can just throw it in the washer. It'll be fine."

I spat back, "It's ruined. It'll stain. It always does."

"It looks fresh. You said it stains when it dries all day. The washer will fix it." He stepped backwards from the doorway, eager to get away from whatever entity had taken over his mother's body.

The vomit did look fresh. The big piles hadn't crusted over yet, but the spatter was dry. I lifted the dress as if it were radioactive, then stomped through the entire house, down the stairs, and into the laundry room, cursing with every step.

I yelled at JJ, "Don't you dare feed the cat. He'll just puke again." (This is standard procedure with any cat vomit incident, not just the traumatizing ones.)

The dress came out of the washer clean, with not a burnt sienna stain to be seen. That did not uplift my mood.

JJ reported the incident to his dad. I could hear their whispers as they planned my intervention.

The next morning before leaving for school, JJ shut my bedroom door. He said as he passed me in the hallway, "That way the cat can't puke on your clothes while you're at work."

I shut the door until the Pandemic when no one left for school or work.

But I've got even another example, worse than the dress. One pre-pandemic summer we drove to Missouri to visit Laura Ingalls Wilder's home and museum. We left plenty of water and food for Kippy, who wouldn't see us again for three days. We shut all bedroom and office doors, but he still had plenty of space to roam and plenty of comfy spots to curl up in the sunshine. After our six-hour drive home, we returned to find an exorbitant amount of puke splattered over half the couch. Had it been blood, the police would still be looking for a body. And the puke was all over the chaise lounge section—*my* spot on the couch.

I'm one of those people who clean the house before going on vacation. The last thing I want to do when I get home from traveling is clean. Other than a couple of loads of laundry from our suitcases, I don't have to do anything after unpacking. I can spend the evening propped with my feet up, relaxing in my clean living room.

The cat puke destroyed everything.

JJ wanted to head out to the airport to do some plane spotting, which had been planned as we pulled into the driveway. They left me home, by myself, as I spent almost an hour scrubbing the couch (between irrational snot-filled sobs I silently thanked my good sense to pay the extra for furniture protective spray, otherwise those burnt sienna splotches would still be seen today). In their defense, I was inconsolable anyway, yet felt oddly abandoned in my time of need. Upon their return, they tiptoed around me, whispering, even suggesting I go to bed early when I made a fuss about not being able to put my feet up because I couldn't sit on the wet couch.

The next time we went on vacation, I draped a blanket over the couch and prepared myself for the worst. If I can anticipate the worst-case scenario, I won't be caught off guard. Part of my hostility is a result of the unpredictable nature of cat vomit, that most unfortunate surprise when you turn the corner.

Let me in advance apologize for the incident you are about to read.

I don't remember the day I had. Maybe teaching students at a juvenile detention center had sucked out every ounce of patience from me that day. Maybe I had personal relationships that were frazzled that day. Maybe my hormones had knocked the shit out of me. Maybe my anxiety had built up for awhile. I don't remember a series of events that made me want to curl up in a ball and cry, like first the dishwasher breaks, then the car malfunctions, and then the roof collapses. It was winter and I was in desperate need of some sun. But I remember feeling drained, unable to escape into my television shows that evening, whatever they might have been. Perhaps the winter monotony had taken its toll for all I wanted to do was crawl into bed. I love my bed. I love snuggling up under my pink microfiber sheets. I love the feel of my head on my fluffy pillow as the foamy mattress pad conforms to my left shoulder and hip. The lingering smell of Febreze and the whir of the fan release all the day's tension from my body.

It was just after nine o'clock and I couldn't keep my eyes open, so I was headed to bed a good hour before Tony would join me. Perhaps I'm just trying to rationalize the descent of my sanity that evening.

When I began to pull the pink comforter back, I saw it, that burnt sienna pile of puke perfectly centered between the two sets of pillows. I threw the comforter down to reveal a second pile of puke between the sheets, the back-side of the comforter with puke on it, as well as both the fitted and flat sheet. It had even sunk through the layers of the foamy mattress pad.

I ranted, yelled, swore as I tore the bed apart. Pillows flew across the room, the mattress pad leaped down the hallway, pillowcases dangled from the ceiling fan. The floor fan fell as I shoved the mattress so I could rip the fitted sheet off the corner. Throw pillows became just that—thrown across the room. The logical side of me must have gotten paper towels to gather the pile of puke and I must have stomped down to the laundry room, but I don't remember doing so. I only remember the angry tears that flowed down my cheeks as I scrubbed the puke out of the comforter with dish soap, yelling to an empty room that my washer wasn't large enough to adequately clean a king-sized comforter. I tried ridiculously to dry it with a kitchen towel. Frustrated with the lack of results, I spent a good five minutes whipping that poor kitchen towel on the comforter as though I was trying to kill a fly and didn't have a fly swatter to do so. I stomped my feet as I tore through the linen closet, digging out plum-colored sheets that hadn't been used for years. They still smelled of hot cardboard from my move a few years before. The only comforters I had in my closet were twin size.

Although JJ had disappeared downstairs to his room an hour before, he could hear my temper tantrum. Conversations travel ceaselessly through the vents. He didn't have to see my meltdown. My next-door neighbors might have even heard it.

Tony was busy on his computer with a pressing work issue. All he said was, "I'll take care of it when I'm done. Go watch some TV." No one understood that I wanted to go to bed *right now*. It would take over an hour for my sheets to wash and dry, never mind the wet spots on the comforter.

I continued swearing as I remade the bed with the god-awful sheets. I chose the twin-sized purple satin comforter I had bought for Mom when her cancer worsened and she slept on a hospital bed out in the living room (she said the color and design made her happy, which did not have that effect on me at this ridiculously trying moment in my life). I threw the mattress pad in the garage and told the cat I better not see him any time soon. He sat like an Egyptian statue and blinked his big innocent cat eyes at me.

I slept like shit without my foamy mattress pad. I shivered as I tried to fall asleep to the smell of old cardboard. All I wanted was to crawl into my perfect bed and go to sleep. Surely that must not be too much to ask for.

When I woke the next morning, the icky sheets reminded me immediately of the previous night's events. A clearer head prevailed. Too much, perhaps, for a log of regret had settled in my stomach, a weight to carry despite the exorcism sleep had brought me.

I looked at Tony. I sighed. "I guess I overreacted last night."

"Oh good. I was wondering who'd I wake up to this morning. Glad to see it's not that monster from last night."

"It was bad, wasn't it?"

"You think?"

As I hot rolled my hair, Kippy pranced down the hallway, rubbing against every corner. I looked at him. "This is all your fault, you know."

He replied with a squeaky meow.

"Aren't you the least bit sorry? I mean, really, how does one puke *between* the sheets?" I bent down to pet his furry white head.

He purred, which probably translated into *It takes some practice. Wait until you see where I puke next.*

When JJ came upstairs for breakfast, he looked at me as Tony had, like I was Sybil, wondering what personality would greet him this morning.

I took a deep breath. "I would like to apologize for my behavior last night. It was out of line and unnecessary."

JJ just stared back at first. By now he was a sophomore in high school. "You were totally out of control. I don't want to be around you when you get all crazy like that."

"Was it really that bad?"

"You were crazy, and no one could talk any sense into you. You don't need to do that every time the cat pukes."

"I will try to be more level-headed next time."

"Just don't get all crazy. It's not that big of a deal."

Yes it is. But I nodded my head.

The trigger of cat puke no longer brings forth the Exorcist. When Kippy puked going forward, I just grimaced and tried to put it in perspective—at least it wasn't between the sheets.

A BUNNY BABY
INTERLUDE

Baby bunnies ignite my inner child like no other wild animal can. Maybe it's because they scamper all over the backyard or are just within reach on the sidewalk. They're accessible little things, teeny furballs that bounce around as if they magically appeared out of pages in a fairy-tale book.

Watching a baby bunny eat a dandelion is the world's panacea.

The tiny baby's brown bespeckled fur bursts through green blades of grass. I long to pet him—he could fit in the palm of my hand. He stops at a dandelion and plucks it from the ground in one swift motion. Eating the stem first, he chews, his rounded cheeks rotating in circular motion, his whiskers vibrating as the stem shortens and disappears. Then the flower of the dandelion vanishes into his mouth in one quick bite, his cheeks fully round to accommodate its size.

As I watch this, all my fear, anger, resentment, irritation, anxiety, stress…all those vanish as if there was no need to name them in the first place, replaced with only serenity and joy. No pill, no drug, no coping mechanism would ever be needed in a world where one could watch baby bunnies eat dandelions all day long.

THE CAT WHISPERER

Sleeping Beauty is more a fitting moniker for Tony than it is for me.

I stink in the animal world. My fruity or musky lotions, my hairspray, my nail polish probably all inflame the sensitive snouts of pets across the land. (Yet every pet I've owned loves to smell the mascara on my eyelashes.) And deep inside of me, a Lennie lives, where I want to pet and squeeze and snuggle any furry creature within arm's reach. Their supersoft heads are my favorite, which turns me into a predatory animal.

Tony won't even make eye contact and animals come running.

I'm sure Kippy thought Tony was another cat. I took such favoritism personally.

Kippy and Tony developed an unhealthy relationship. I'd even call it disgusting.

I could call for Kippy and he would remain wherever he was, doing whatever he was doing. Tony would only have to make his cat call, a cross between a meow and a Chewbacca vibrato, and Kippy would come running from downstairs, a deep sleep, or even from his dish full of Fancy Feast.

Kippy kept a keen ear of our whereabouts. If he heard me join Tony on the couch for a late afternoon snuggle, he'd suddenly appear in the living room. I laid on top of Tony, with my head on his chest, so Kippy would have to settle for piling on my back. The pressure of his little paws on my spine was better than any spa massage; sometimes he'd even make biscuits. Most of the time though, he'd crawl over me, his back clawed paws sinking into the squishy flesh of my neck, so he could be nose-to-nose with Tony. Other times he'd bypass my back, finding a tiny spot between my shoulder and Tony's cheek, intent on fitting there, squeezing me off the couch.

Kippy rubbed himself against Tony's arms and legs, but especially liked Tony's five o'clock shadow. I should be happy Kippy didn't want to rub himself all over the half dozen whiskers I continually plucked from my chin, but I still felt left out of their blatant bond. Kippy purred before he even jumped on Tony. Tony would push Kippy away, his stubble laced with white cat hairs, as if he was in the beginning phase of turning into the Abominable Snowman. Then Kippy would jump onto the back of the chair or couch and start licking Tony's crew cut. This would continue long enough for Tony to feel the burn of Kippy's sandpaper tongue.

Once the Pandemic hit, Tony worked remotely and never had to return to the office, so Kippy grew accustomed to Tony's constant presence. After he spent some time bathing in the morning sun that streamed through our living room windows, Kippy would walk back to Tony's office to nap in there. Every time Tony stood up, Kippy followed. Because Tony usually gave Kippy a treat whenever he went out to smoke, he teased Kippy at times, walking into the hallway, then just returning to his office.

I was left out of their little games.

Every time Tony lay on the couch to dink around on his phone, Kippy joined him, jumping on his chest to stare into Tony's eyes. Kippy despised Tony's phone, attempting to position himself between Tony's hands and chin, squeezing himself between Tony and the phone. I'd hear Tony say, "Leave me alone" or "Quit following me."

I think Tony loved having someone adore him so much.

Tony needed one of those kangaroo pouches that parents use to swaddle their new babies, a hands-free solution to a needy infant. Kippy would have loved such a contraption, never leaving Tony's side yet free to nap at his desire.

Kippy would seek me out from time to time, usually finding me on my computer in my office. He stared at me, telepathically telling me to make room for him on my lap. He never stayed for long, eventually settling on my trunk in my office. He liked the register that blew warm air behind it. He would nestle on my chest if I sat on the chaise in the library, where he'd purr as the spring sun stretched through the windows. Because Kippy was a big cat, he never sat comfortably in my arms. I wanted to carry him like a baby—over my shoulder—while Tony carried him like a newborn cradled in his arms, with Kippy on his back. Yet all cats are too small to hug. Instead, I rubbed foreheads with Kippy, leaving bronze powder behind on his white fur.

But I was always second choice.

If Tony wasn't home, Kippy would wait to join me on

the couch as if out of contempt. I could call him repeatedly, but he ignored me. He would only jump on my lap after realizing Tony was not returning. Instead of snuggling with me on my belly staring into my eyes, he turned his butt to me, laying on my knees.

Tony attracts all animals. They don't mind his cologne or whether he shaves or not or the cigarette smoke that lingers on his skin and clothes—they flock to him as if he is their leader or some godlike entity that they must sniff. He even fed a squirrel a peanut from his hand—multiple times. I have never been so jealous of anyone in my life. Yet he's the one that complains about all the babies. He's the one that yells at them more than I do. He tosses them off his lap. And even chooses his phone over Kippy.

Yet they love him more.

Tony was the one destined to be Sleeping Beauty.

KIPPY THE CAT-DOG

The perfect pet: one who possesses the training and intuitiveness of a dog, but with the low-maintenance and personality of a cat.

Kippy was the perfect pet.

We trained Kippy to put himself to bed. He knew what "night night" meant, jumping down from our laps to retire to his bed in the basement. After waking up in the middle of the night too many times to a vibrating mattress as Kippy cleaned himself at two in the morning, Kippy was forced to sleep downstairs. Kippy learned to jiggle the pocket door open—had he stayed out of our room, he could have slept anywhere upstairs. But he always headed for our bedroom. Tony said a fly fart would wake me, so Kippy was doomed. We wedged a folded paper towel into the far end of the pocket door so Kippy couldn't wiggle it to get it open. He'd rattle the door in the mornings, demanding attention and his breakfast.

Much like a dog, Kippy awaited my arrival home from lunch and greeted me by the door. He also stalked the mailman and lurched for the window during package deliveries. If I told him Papa's home, Kippy walked coolly to the door, nonchalantly, although inside I think he was bursting with joy like a hyperactive puppy.

Although Kippy didn't bark when we said "speak," he did meow to our questions. In his later years, Kippy became much more vocal, much to my delight. If I asked, "Are you hungry?" Kippy replied, "Meow." "Do you want to help me with the laundry?" Meow. "What should Momma do today?" Meow. I never figured out what *meow* meant as an activity. When his meow would come out as more of a squeak, Tony would ask him, "Did you break your squeaker?" Silent Meow.

Sometimes Kippy's meows were the demanding sort, like the kind he used in the mornings when he wanted his Fancy Feast Gravy Lovers. Or when I opened a pouch of tuna for lunch. Or when he stood at the backdoor and looked at me while I sat outside. Other times, his meows were soft, as if he was saying how much he loved us. These softer meows he saved for Snuggle Time.

Kippy's favorite time of day and most favorite thing in the world was Snuggle Time (his second favorite was walking on still-wet mopped floors, leaving kitty pawprints on my Swiffered floor). Most nights, Tony and I would plop on the couch by eight o'clock, thus officially beginning Snuggle Time. Kippy would run out from wherever he was and jump onto Tony's lap. He'd stay with us all night long—more so with Tony than with me.

Like a dog (minus the drool), Kippy craved certain people food.

Blueberry muffins would bring Kippy out of a deep

slumber. He looked forward to weekend mornings with donuts. Although he loved Cheetos, because what animal doesn't, Kippy preferred Tostitos, shoving his head into the bag and plucking out a salty chip.

The only downside to a cat who acts like a dog: Suitcase Anxiety.

Suitcases were once fun, soft-like boxes to root around in, especially within all the shirts, dresses, socks, and under-wear that we packed inside. Even if we shut the lid but left it unzipped, we'd find Kippy curled up inside our suitcase, covering our travel clothes with a layer of white cat hair. JJ couldn't even leave his school backpack open, for Kippy would jump inside it. In his later days, he knew what those suitcases symbolized: an indeterminate number of days without Snuggle Time.

He suspected something nefarious happening behind any closed door. His paw would appear underneath the door, moving sporadically back and forth to find that secret latch to open it. We waited until Kippy was out of sight, perhaps using the bathroom, then took our suitcases from the bottom of the linen closet and shut our bedroom door as we packed. Then we had to hide the suitcases until we left.

But Kippy was too smart for that. Our linen closet had a narrow door, about half an accordion style closet door. Instead of a doorknob, it had a magnetic latch that kept it shut, so it simply pulled open. The gap on the bottom of the door was big enough for Kippy to get his paw under, then he'd pop the door open and root around inside, which became part of his morning rounds: make sure the suitcases were still at the bottom of the closet. If he didn't see them in there, he'd look at us accusingly, following us around until he found the missing suitcase.

Even if just one of us was leaving, Kippy wasn't happy, although he preferred Tony to stay over me.

Because Kippy had turned into a dog, I gave walks a shot again, to no avail. He let me put the harness on him and walked a couple feet down the driveway. Then a car drove by, reducing his bones to mush. His whole body turned to Jell-O, and he melted out of his harness and dashed into the neighbor's yard.

I should have considered any PTSD he might have suffered from his nine months at the lake house. Or the one time I took him to Petco to see Santa, who received a hiss. Kippy probably said "Fuck you" instead of "Cheese" when I took his picture on Santa's lap.

Even the pet stroller failed—Kippy hissed at me, which is something he never did to family members. He spent the rest of our walk meowing in pain and distress. He did not enjoy one step. The ninety-dollar stroller ended up in the donate pile after just one use. I hated going for walks by myself and thought the cat would be a good companion. It was not to be.

Minus his refusal to go on walks, Kippy was everything I thought a cat should be all those years ago, as if I had dreamed him up when I was six.

GOODBYE, KIPPY

About nine months after our family reunited, Kippy stopped eating. He had thrown up several times the days before, which was not that unusual. He always went through cat vomit periods. We'd have no issues except a furball or two for months, and then every day for what seemed like an eternity he'd be puking up that burnt sienna half-digested food. But when he stopped eating, I worried.

Kippy also looked frumpy. He stopped cleaning himself, looking like a hobo cat from New York City as he walked around the house without any giddy-up in his step. Then I found black tar-like poop in the laundry room, even though his litter box sat just steps away.

After a six-hundred-dollar vet bill, they couldn't find anything wrong with Kippy. A couple of days later, Kippy started eating again, as if nothing was wrong.

This would happen about once a year. I still have no answer as to what was wrong with him. It would last about a week, and then he would return to his normal self.

In October, just shy of his fourteenth birthday, he

stopped eating again. The same pattern occurred and at first we thought nothing of it. But due to his age, Tony and I would say an off-handed comment about how Kippy couldn't live forever. I didn't believe it exactly, but Kippy was old. Some cats live until they're twenty, and I assumed Kippy, with his life experiences, would fall into that category.

This time, Kippy's mysterious illness lasted almost two weeks. Just about the time I was going to take him to the vet, he started eating.

And then the week before Thanksgiving, he stopped eating again.

I tried not to panic, yet this time it felt like something was off. Kippy never had these bouts back-to-back.

Tony and I prepared ourselves for the inevitable. We hoped one morning we would find Kippy forever asleep, having died peacefully overnight. I didn't want him to be in pain. He still snuggled with us, jumped on the furniture, and used his litter box.

The wait began.

Kippy noticeably lost weight. He nibbled on donuts Wednesday morning before Thanksgiving. But the stairs to the basement—and his litter box—seemed too much for him. When we found a pee spot on the living room carpet, we moved his litter box upstairs into Tony's office. He still followed us around, but with much less gusto. Snuggle Time became more painful. He couldn't sit comfortably on our laps, preferring to sleep in his Buddha position, perched with his feet curled underneath him.

We debated about taking him to the vet. Since Kippy despised traveling, I feared that would cause more harm.

The stress alone might kill him.

Friday morning, I woke to find him sitting on the corner of the carpet, staring at me. He squeaked a meow, which I hadn't heard in days. I bounded out of bed and snuggled with him on the floor, where he gloriously purred. Flashes of McSteamy's last *Grey's Anatomy* episode kept my hope from growing too much.

The Friday after Thanksgiving meant my house transformed into a Christmas wonderland, including Kippy's beloved tree skirt. Kippy didn't have the strength to follow me to the basement to get underfoot as I took out decorations from the closet under the stairs, instead squeezing between the toilet and the bathroom wall. He hadn't slept there for days, even though it was a favorite spot in the winter, right underneath a flow of warm air from the vent. Even though I usually put the main tree up last, I dug out the tree skirt and laid it on the floor. When Kippy woke up from his bathroom nap, he found me in the living room, curled up on the tree skirt, and slept.

That would be the last time he slept.

Kippy returned to his buddha pose, his nose touching the floor as he tried to sleep. As soon as his head bowed, he'd wake up. He spent the rest of the evening sitting up. He'd lean to one side as if that was the only way he could breathe or the only way he wasn't in pain.

I had flashbacks of Mom, crumpled over in her hospice bed, for that was the only way she could breathe. No one ever prepares you for that—you think when the time comes, people are supine, comfortably in bed, falling asleep to never wake.

It doesn't happen that way.

The last time I saw my mom, I rubbed her skeletal back as she fell asleep, bent over, her head on top of a pillow that sat on her knees. That's how I left my mother; she died that night, probably in that position.

Now Kippy couldn't breathe unless he sat up, meaning he couldn't sleep. It was almost ten o'clock. We fashioned a bed of pillows and blankets next to the trunk at the end of the bed, trying to get him to lean against it so he could sleep. I sat with him on the floor in the middle of the night, hoping he could sleep if he leaned against me. But he didn't want me near him.

In the morning, we found Kippy sitting in our room. I watched as his eyes drooped, as his body slid to the side, desiring nothing but to sleep, the pain jolting him awake.

The time had come.

I sat with Kippy in the hallway, tears in my eyes as I said goodbye. I felt his fur, my fingers committing to memory the feel of his soft white hair. We woke up JJ so he could say goodbye.

Tony was adamant: "I'm not going in the room with you. I can't do that again."

I nodded. I wasn't going to let Kippy die alone. I didn't know if I could handle it either, but with no prior experience, I knew not what was about to happen.

Tony wrapped Kippy in my pink blanket with the gray and white cats on it, creating a pouch-like bed to carry Kippy as comfortably as possible. We didn't want to bring out the pet carrier we had used when we moved to Iowa, then when Kippy went to Minnesota, then when he came back to South Dakota. I didn't want his last moments on earth to be one of an activity he feared and despised.

Tony held Kippy and I drove. Kippy did well until we stopped at a red light. Because it was the Saturday after Thanksgiving, there was too much traffic for me to run it. Kippy started to struggle in Tony's arms and only settled once we exited the car.

The receptionist took one look at Kippy and convinced me, "It's time." *There it is again.* I wanted a vet to look at Kippy first—what if it was curable? What if a magic medicine could heal him? The vet nurse looked sympathetic but told me the harsh reality: "We'd have to give him oxygen and that would put him in distress."

We were moved to the front of the line, brought back immediately, and filled out the necessary paperwork.

Tony let Kippy down, where he crawled around haggardly, still appearing curious. It was the most active we'd seen him in 24 hours. The vet nurse came in and manhandled Kippy, setting him on the table. I wanted to interject, to tell her that Kippy couldn't breathe if she held him like that, but she had Kippy on the table in seconds.

Tony wrapped Kippy back up in the blanket. The vet nurse asked if we were staying. "I am," I said as I sucked in my tears. Tony saw my face and said, "I'll stay."

The nurse picked up Kippy again. "We'll put in a stint and bring her right back."

Before I could say anything, she disappeared behind the door. Wouldn't that put him in distress, which was what we were all trying to avoid? We heard a hissy meow and in seconds the nurse opened the door, placing a frozen Kippy on the table.

He was already dead.

Apparently he bit someone, going out with a fight.

Sobs exploded from my chest. This was what we had tried to avoid. We didn't want Kippy to suffer, yet his last moments on earth were ones of fear, pain, and without the comfort of me or Tony.

Kippy's frozen face was all I could see: his mouth was open, enough to expose his fangs. His pupils were dilated, his eyes wide. I pet him nonetheless, as the nurse tried to explain that his heart was still beating faintly, as if that meant something now.

Kippy's body jolted, which made me jump. I continued to pet his side as snot ran from my nose and mascara stained my face.

The nurse was apologetic, knowing that this was not the peaceful death that was promised and expected. "I wanted to rush her back in here so you could be with her." I didn't hear the rest, but wanted to lash out and say HIM, not her. I berated myself for letting Kippy die like this. If he was so close to death, we should have let him die at home. We should have held him until his last breath, but I was so afraid he'd be in pain. And now he died like this.

I remained sitting there, sobbing as the nurse told us that Kippy was officially dead, his heart had stopped. She left us alone as I continued to cry. The tears pooled and puddled into my cakey eyelashes, the floor only a gray iridescent blob, as my fingers touched Kippy's fur for the last time.

I don't remember what Tony said, only that at one point he stroked my hair. I continued to mumble, incomprehensible, "This wasn't supposed to happen."

The vet nurse returned, hesitant. Tony knew I could sit there for the foreseeable future; he took my arm to help me up. The nurse finally spoke. "Do you want me to take the blanket with her?"

I hadn't expected this. I nodded, parting with the pink blanket covered in cats, the one I bought last spring to use between my Valentine kitty blanket and the black cat Halloween blanket. Kippy loved my blankets; I hoped it would bring him comfort wherever he was.

We left with nothing but regret and blame and guilt.

I don't remember that afternoon, only hearing Tony go in and out of the garage a couple of times. He threw Kippy's litter box and water fountain dish in the trash. The spot beside the fridge, right around the corner of the back entryway, was noticeably empty. A staple that had been there for seven years, now void. I think I finished decorating, but I can't remember. It didn't feel right to blare my Christmas music—I only remember the silence of the house as I strung beads on the tree without a cat chasing, pawing, and pulling on the other end.

I held back tears that evening during Snuggle Time. I would say more to myself than anyone, "I miss Kippy." I should have let him go outside more for he loved it so much.

I would have trouble falling asleep for days. I could only see Kippy's frozen face when I shut my eyes.

HELLO, BABY

I hated the emptiness in the house. No furry critter under-foot, no tiny footprints on my freshly mopped floors, and no little dishes beside the refrigerator.

I tried to find the upside of a pet-free home. I no longer had to vacuum cat hair from the furniture, which halved my cleaning time. I saved money—no more expensive cans of Fancy Feast, which went up in price every time I went to Walmart or Target. My feet stayed kitty litter free when I walked in the laundry room to switch loads. And the best: no more surprise piles of cat vomit.

But I would have traded all that for Snuggle Time on the couch again. For the comic relief, the peace and content-ment an animal always brought to my home. The sound of meows and purrs, stealthy footprints with just the slight click of claws on tiny paws.

Our home always had an animal in it for the past 23 years (minus that tortuous nine months). Now the void and silence became unbearable.

During the Pandemic, we thought about getting a dog.

I wanted to go for walks so Tony begrudgingly came with me. The Pandemic ended and we still had no dog. Every few months, we would talk about adopting a friend for Kippy, but the exorbitant costs for a dog and insane adoption process kept us from proceeding (times had changed since we bought Ginger over twenty years ago). We even checked out rescue centers and pounds, but all they had were big, angry dogs. Plus, Tony longed for a bear-sized dog, while I wanted a purse-sized one. We shelved the idea, although as homebodies, we had lots of time for a dog.

Three months after Kippy died, I couldn't handle the silence. Even after cleaning the house in record time, plopping on the Febrezed couch with a clean blanket to watch *Survivor* seemed lackluster, like the couch wasn't all that dirty to begin with and it would have felt the same had I not cleaned it. No matter how much we laughed, the house remained somber underneath, a quietly depressing void that hung in the spaces where cat hair used to collect. Our yearly Christmas picture was a first—without a furry baby.

But I realized something that I had inaccurately assumed about myself all my life: I always thought I was more of a dog person than a cat person, or at least equal parts dog and cat person. In reality, I had always been a cat person with a Crazy Cat Lady soul from the time I was born but had grown up in a dog person household.

Tony found munchkin kittens online—I thought I might die from cuteness, despite their outrageous price tag. But it was too soon. Just as I would never have another Pomeranian, adopting another cat soon after Kippy's death was too much for me. Even a black fluffy cat would be too close to Kippy, like I was replacing him. It had to be a dog.

With the realization that I was a cat person, I couldn't insist upon a little lap dog that I could carry around in a purse. So many years ago, Tony had never argued about my dream of a Pomeranian. A big dog it was.

Upon our return from Florida, where we escaped our winter from hell only to return to a blizzard and two more snow days, I stated a fact: "We don't travel that much. We're more at home than away from home. JJ's in college now. Why don't we have a dog?"

The next week, he found a Newfoundland/Great Pyrenees mix for only eight hundred dollars that was just thirty miles away. I pounced on the idea without thinking it through. I used my upcoming birthday as the reason: a puppy would make the perfect gift.

I knew if we sat on the decision, debated it, or even waited another day, we probably would decide against it. I embraced our younger selves, when we bought Ginger without thinking, when I snuck out in the afternoon and found Kippy despite the chaos in my life. Why shouldn't we get a dog? No matter the responsibility, mess, or cost, I knew a dog would bring us joy no matter what.

The next morning we drove to pick up our new baby. Life as we knew it would change, and maybe not all for the better. More responsibility. More expenses. Less freedom. Such thoughts never occurred to us 24 years ago when we drove to meet Ginger. During the thirty-minute drive, Tony said, "We can still back out. Are you sure you want to do this?"

No, I wasn't. I wanted a kitty cat. But I knew he wanted a dog. A big dog. And fate had placed these puppies within our space and time. It was meant to be.

We pulled into the dirt driveway of what appeared to be a large breeding farm, with fenced kennels all around the house. The lady ushered us inside. The smell of dog brought tears to my eyes, the noxious stink suffocating my lungs.

All the puppies napped in the living room inside a kenneled area in front of a worn-out sectional and beside an unorganized office area. They slept around the perimeter, some stretched out and others curled up, one white and black puppy blending into the next.

I felt my childhood heart beat again.

No space allowed for me to imitate Mom. Eight large puppies with me in the middle meant I was already touching half the puppies. Some came to sniff me, but most continued sleeping. Not what I expected.

Even though Tony wanted a male because those grew even bigger than females, I wanted a girl. We had both fallen in love with the green collar of the litter. She had a symmetrical face: the black ears and black sides of her head were divided by a white stripe of fur almost centered in her forehead. She was predominantly white, with two large black patches near her butt. Tony picked her up and she snuggled with him. He handed her to me and that was that.

She felt heavy on my lap as we drove home in a blizzard, for snow had started falling and the wind made the roads treacherous. She already weighed more than Kippy and Ginger combined, but she sat quietly while we drove home, curious but anxious.

We had toyed with dog names earlier, agreeing on Panda since her size and coloring would match that of the bear, yet our puppy was more white than black, her face not giving me Panda vibes. I suggested Baby because that's what

I called all the animals I saw. (And I couldn't help thinking, "No one puts Baby in a corner.") It would become ironic as she grew—nothing about her would be babyish.

"Why not Baby?"

Tony grimaced. "She's your puppy, so go ahead and call her Baby."

Her name was the only thing about her that would be mine. Tony would spend the first couple weeks apologetically revealing her name whenever people asked, making sure they knew it wasn't his idea. But most women and girls swooned over the name.

Our home no longer felt empty once we brought Baby home.

The afternoon of her adoption, I ran around in the house with Baby while Tony drove JJ back to college on snowy roads. By the time Tony returned, Baby had collapsed, sleeping soundly, not even acknowledging Tony. It was cute to see Tony upset. "You got to play with her all afternoon."

I would experience more joy out of watching Tony interact with Baby than having a new puppy in the house. "You're such a good puppy!" as he rubbed her sides. "Give Papa kisses" as he rolled around with her on the floor. His high-pitched tone was the same one he used for baby JJ all those years ago. After we had Baby for six months, when she had been gone all morning to a grooming appointment, Tony said, "I miss my Baby."

PET CEMETERY

No, not that Pet Sematary.

After Mom died, Dad eventually moved back to Iowa, building a new house on Mom's family land. As an only child, Mom kept all her dad's farmland, but sold the acreage with his house and the barn. Dad's new house sat on the other side of the thick patch of trees near the road. From his sliding glass door, we could see the small area of land down the hill that used to be the cane mill. Old trees dotted the area, keeping it concealed from the side gravel road. Dad turned this area into a pet cemetery.

Before he moved, Dad dug up Elsa's box from under the deck. Ginger had died, and a couple years later, my sister's dog, Savannah, died. We already had three family dogs for the cemetery.

With the help of his brother, Dad cleared dead trees and branches and set up a wrought iron fence around a small plot of cleared land. He placed Mom's stone bench that had once sat in our backyard outside the cemetery fence.

Old trees sheltered the cemetery's inhabitants, the sun

shining between their branches. Birds chirping within the white noise of wind rippling through leaves became the soundtrack for the cemetery, offering a quiet respite to all who visited. Although Ginger and Savannah had never traipsed around on the land, we knew all three would approve of their final resting spot.

At first, I wanted to keep Ginger's ashes in the built-in opposite my dining room. But as I aged, mortality became a nearer reality. By now, Mom had died seven years before, and with Dad's move, even more of Mom's stuff had been parted up, given away, or reorganized in totes and trunks.

I thought of my own stuff. What would my son do with all my junk? I started donating items I never thought I would. I condensed totes with only those items I could use and displayed beloved keepsakes. I donated many of my stuffed animals, apologizing to my inner child who didn't understand.

Ginger's keepsake box sat in my hallway built-in, whose glass doors displayed my beloved items. After she died, I kept some of her toys and her clothes: Pocahantas, SpongeBob, her Jan Brady sweater, her Petco bows. I donated some of the Pomeranian figurines I had collected over the years, keeping only a couple. I pondered the state of her ashes. JJ would save those, but whether he found a good spot to keep them safe I couldn't be sure. If JJ married and had a family of his own, would his kids—my grandkids—take care of those ashes? Ginger would be left with complete strangers. I feared she would end up in a landfill or a thrift store, an unbearable thought.

Having her in a permanent spot away from me was better than having her near me for the rest of my life. I needed her to find a forever home, one for eternity, not just a temporary place with me (although I did ponder why she couldn't be buried with me—why don't people do that?).

A granite plaque with Ginger's engraved picture marked her grave, which would provide context to what pet was buried there should anyone in an apocalyptic future stumble upon that little fenced cemetery.

Dad had made a wooden cross for Elsa, which he said was temporary until we figured out something else for gravestones. We buried Ginger next to Elsa, and Savannah was buried on the other side of Ginger.

When Mom died, I became the designated maker of Memorial Day flowers. Every member of my family was buried in my grandparents' town: Mom, both sets of grandparents, an aunt, and an uncle I never knew who died of scarlet fever at eight years old. Mom had wanted to be buried in South Dakota, but Dad convinced her otherwise. She thought no one would visit if she were buried in Iowa, but Dad promised he would go often, not realizing he would move there three years after she died. Once a week he puts a fresh pink rose on her grave, even thirteen years later.

I visit every Memorial Day, with flowers to decorate all the graves. And now I make three more for our pet cemetery.

When I returned later that summer, the pet cemetery had a haunted vibe to it. All the flower bouquets had spiderwebs covering them and the flowers looked weathered and worn, faded and windblown. Yet the little cemetery held a serenity I couldn't find anywhere else in the world, a gothic Victorian ambiance as though it had been preserved for over a hundred years, haunted only by friendly ghosts and fond memories.

Because I create a Christmas spread for Mom's monument every holiday, I bought red poinsettia garland for Dad to drape around the fence of the pet cemetery. He later added a wreath with solar powered lights to hang on the gate.

Kippy joined Elsa, Ginger, and Savannah at the pet cemetery. We buried him in front of Ginger, marking his grave with a picture-engraved plaque.

Dad and I finally decided on metal crosses for all the pets. Dad welded them and painted them white. I adhered letters to the crosses for each one, spelling out the name to sparkle in the sun. I wish I could say that the pet cemetery was complete, but Baby will end up there too.

A RED, SPLOTCHY MESS

Throughout my life, I've developed allergies to things I once used or ate for years without issue, like Cherry ChapStick, penicillin, and fresh fruit and vegetables. It's like my body was fine with whatever synthetic or natural substance my body absorbed and then decided nope, no more.

During college, when I came home for holidays, Elsa became my new allergy.

Giving Elsa hugs and kisses would give me itchy watery eyes and bumpy scratchy wrists. By day two, I would come out of it. When little bumps appeared, I didn't scratch them; they would disappear in a couple of hours if I left them alone. Allergies would never keep me from snuggling with my furry sister.

Ginger's paw pads left little red puffy welts on my arms. If her wet nose kissed my face, a bump would immediately appear. If I didn't itch it, it would vanish in an hour or so.

Pet dander clogged my sinuses, causing sneezes and stuffiness. I used to brush Ginger all the time when she was little because she'd get clumpies behind her ears and under her arms. I had to bring her to Petco when I couldn't handle my congestion anymore. The wet dog shampoo smell inflamed my eyes and burned my chest. If I had to wait for Ginger, I'd stand outside because I would start to feel my nose clog and my eyes water within seconds.

Kippy's paw pads did the same as Ginger's: left itchy blotches on my skin. If his nose touched my chest, he left a welt behind. Because Kippy shed all the time, I invested in carpenter masks when I deep cleaned. If I moved furniture, washed curtains, organized the linen closet, or vacuumed both sides of the couch cushions, a mask saved me from a night of misery (this was long before the Pandemic).

My son inherited my blotchiness. I told him almost every day when he was little: "Don't roll around with the cat. You're going to get all blotchy." His face and neck would show telltale signs of my genetics: red splotches appeared immediately (not to mention the cat hair that covered his clothes).

As I've aged, I've grown more sensitive. Watermelon and strawberries cause feverish hives (I miss watermelon dearly), lipsticks and mascaras with any sort of plumpers or fillers cause itchy puffiness, and even cleaning supplies like the orange and green Clorox wipes leave my hands burning hot long after I've washed them. Forest fire smoke makes me wheeze for days and windy days make me sneeze uncontrollably.

When we brought Baby home, I worried how my skin and nose would respond. After we had her for a day, my chest tightened and my throat felt scratchy, like I was coming down with something. My nose dripped when I bent over, while one side clogged up at night. After three days, it cleared. Her big paws don't seem to bother me, which is fortunate, considering the size of the welt they would leave behind. I adore giving her bearhugs daily, despite the blotchiness left behind on my neck.

All in the name of love.

MO' PUPPY, MO' PROBLEMS

❝Why do you want a big dog so bad?" This was the question I asked Tony in our cyclic conversations about getting a dog.

His constant reply: "They're gentle giants."

My retort: "And they could crush us."

I listed all the ways a big dog would cause more problems than a little lap dog.

"Think about how much more dog food you're going to have to buy."

"They don't eat that much once they get older."

"That doesn't make any sense."

How it turned out: Baby eats a hell of a lot more food than Kippy and Ginger combined. But Baby won't even eat dog food, once she realized that was not what was on our plates. We have to plan for a third portion or make her something different if we eat a meal that isn't dog friendly. Tony even orders her meals whenever we eat out. As we're debating what's for supper, he'll say, "But Baby won't eat that." She's more finicky than I am and much more unpredictable. She'll refuse donuts for weeks only to salivate for them later. Tony and I are always hungry now, since we give her half of our people food. If we have leftovers, Baby usually eats them.

"No more Snuggle Time."
"She can be a lap dog."
"How is that possible?"
How it turned out: Baby thinks she's a lap dog. Her heavy paws feel like they can crush my chest. She cannot make biscuits, instead she's crushing crab shells. I can't see past her big head to watch television when she decides to plop on my legs. If I snuggle with Tony, I risk having a huge paw claw me in the face. She crushes her body up against my legs and I cannot resituate myself or the blanket. Her elbows are knives that dig into my thighs. Tony tells her every time she jumps on his lap, "You're just a little lap dog!"

"She's going to destroy the furniture."
"Why would she do that?"
"Because she's going to weigh over a hundred pounds."
How it turned out: Baby hasn't destroyed my couch and library chaise—yet—but her sasquatch paws and claws have left their marks like Freddy Kreuger loose in a furniture store. Her claws wrecked the living room window screen—I fear she'll break the window as she paws at it in her excitement upon our arrival home or of the potential danger of neighbors snow blowing their driveways. My couch cushions have sunk beneath Baby's weight, and the seams in my

library chaise widen a millimeter a day.

"There's no room for her to sleep in bed with us."

"There's plenty of room for her."

"We have a queen-sized bed. And if I banished Kippy to the basement, there's no way I'm going to be able to sleep with an adult-sized dog."

How it turned out: Tony placed Baby in bed with us a couple of times if she woke up too early. Even as a puppy, she hogged the bed, rolled around constantly, and used all parts of my body as a pillow. Now she wanders around the house at night. Her feet are not stealthy like cat paws but sound more like a Clydesdale without the jingle bells. When she lies down, it's like a cow falling over while having a seizure. She talks in her sleep, whining and yipping, and she flails her big paws about, scratching whatever wall or door she's lying up against. Now that she's aged, she's content to sleep on the floor, only joining us on the bed after five in the morning. She sits in between us and stares, like the dog version of *Paranormal Activity*. Once she is satisfied that we are still breathing, she turns herself around and plops by our feet.

"What are you going to do when she's tall enough to reach the counters? Or any other shelves in the house for that matter?"

Tony shrugs. "I have found on TikTok these dogs like to sleep on countertops."

"What?"

How it turned out: Baby stood next to me in the bathroom with her front paws on the vanity. She took her leash off the kitchen counter. She snatched her brushes from Tony's office. She knocked over plates of food on the edge of the counter. And while we ate, she stole the roast we left on the counter (so much for leftovers).

"How am I going to walk such a big dog?"
"They're gentle giants."
"Stop saying that."
How it turned out: When Baby was about fifty pounds, our walk went well, until she decided to train for professional cotton catcher. She about pulled my arm off to chase a floating white fluff in the wind. As she's aged, she's become calmer, but still too unpredictable. I don't trust her should we meet another dog, a person, a butterfly, a bicyclist, a motorcycle, a bunny, a squirrel…did I mention blowing cotton? I don't walk her, much to my dismay.

And one situation I never considered: drool.
The puddles of water after Baby drinks from her dish could rot my floor. Then she leaves a trail of drips throughout the house. CSI markers could trace the drool spatter from the crime scene all the way to her getaway. It's worse when she uses my dress as a napkin, leaving a drool spot so big it looks like I wet myself.
My favorite thing about her largeness: the hugs.
Ginger was too small for bear hugs, yet Baby reminds me of my childhood Elsa hugs. I hug Baby dozens of times a day because who wouldn't want doggie hugs? I rub foreheads with her too. (The smell of a dog or cat forehead is comparable to a baby's—JJ's head smelled of a muted vanilla with a hint of baby powder, fresh and clean; Baby's

head smells like Kippy's did, a musky vanilla with earthy undertones.)

We've acclimated to Baby's size, not realizing how big she is until we see her next to another large dog. Tony thinks she's not growing enough. He suffers from DDD: dog dysmorphic disorder.

Whenever Tony complains about anything that I think relates to Baby's size, I remind him: "Mo' puppy, mo' problems."

CRAZY CAT LADY

I imagine myself as an old lady, in a house with gawdy furniture, outdated décor, with cats. Lots of cats. Everywhere. While I'm wearing a shirt with cats on it.

I forgot how sensitive dogs are. Both dogs and cats have their temperamental moments, especially while you dye your hair or put on a hat—they react like Stranger Danger. But dogs pout until you apologize. It's like dealing with a person, which is precisely why I prefer animals to people. They don't behave like people, but dogs pouting equates to dealing with conflict, which I avoid.

Baby, like most puppies, suffered from the Zoomies. Once those started, I couldn't redirect her. I clapped my hands or yelled "stop" to get her attention, but she thought I was playing. I scolded her and she ignored me. One time, she wanted to dance with me in my cramped bathroom, almost knocking me into the tub. I pushed her out of the bathroom and shut the door.

To which she pouted.

She sulked the rest of the night. I asked her to sit with

me on the couch, but she walked away, plopping down on the floor behind the couch. A derisive sigh escaped her mouth as she slid her paws out in front of her.

She'll pout, I'll eventually apologize, and it's this whole drama until we kiss and make up—literally, for she gives me kisses although I prefer hugs. Dogs behave like perpetual toddlers. Baby steals socks and dryer sheets out of the laundry room just so we chase her, so she has our full attention. Just like a toddler who knows the fastest way to get a parent's attention is through naughtiness. Cats act more like passive aggressive teenagers.

They don't pout. You yell at them, and they look at you. Then they walk away, probably mumbling "Whatever" under their breaths like a moody teenager. Despite all that I've read online about cats holding grudges, Kippy didn't. He maybe never forgot, but once we both went to our separate corners, we'd meet back up again and all was fine.

But maybe it's his reaction I preferred. Kippy stood on his hind legs, front paws on the screen door, meowing at me and giving me a dirty look as I read on the deck while he served his day of grounding for climbing a tree after a squirrel. Eventually he'd entertain himself or fall asleep. He might have been aloof to me later, but since he openly preferred Tony over me, I couldn't tell anyway.

I enjoy the low maintenance of a cat because even needy cats aren't as high-strung as dogs.

One can leave the house for a couple of days without finding a babysitter or a kennel. I worried about Kippy even if we took a day road trip. He hated being by himself for extended periods of time, but it's not like we were always gone. I left him heart-shaped bowls filled with treats throughout the house, giving him little surprises to find to break up his alone time.

One can always pick up a cat. I think, anyway. (I've seen way too many obese cats on TikTok though, so maybe not.) Cats can sit on laps—they're easy enough to shove off laps if need be, too.

Cats prefer warmth to cold. Dogs boil in seconds, preferring shade to sun. I'm always cold, except if I'm suffering from a hot flash, so I want a warm furry body on my lap. Baby is panting within seconds unless she has a fan pointed at her. She will lie next to me at night on the couch, but not for long, for she prefers the cool hardwood floor.

Cats are almost noiseless. Yet their meows and purrs are the most delightful sounds on earth. Whenever Kippy purred as I pet him, I felt my anxiety and stress diminish. I loved talking to Kippy, especially the phrases he knew that would get him to meow. "Do you want to go outside?" Meow. "You want your breakfast?" Meow. "What should we have for supper?" Tuna.

Dogs' barks grate on my ears, persistent and echoing as they threaten to trigger a migraine. Yet Baby's playtime yips and gargles always make me giggle.

Who doesn't love a slobbery dog kiss, or a snout pushed into your palm (but not your crotch)? But nothing beats a cat making biscuits on your chest or your leg or your arm, a gentle massage with a purring soundtrack.

Maybe our preference comes from how we see ourselves. If we prefer to chase our own tails than to make biscuits, perhaps we're a dog person. If we prefer to bask in the sun rather than eat in the shade, perhaps we're a cat person.

WHO'S MY BABY?

Baby stares at me as I sit on the couch. Or stares at me as I write. Or stares at me as I stand in the bathroom in front of the mirror. I look at her. "What do you want?"

An intense look is the reply until I move. Then Baby walks away from me, every other step turning her head around to make eye contact, to communicate with me that I must keep walking, following her. Her head swings from one side to the next, her size now that of a pony, her tail swishing as each step swivels her hips. Her wishful eyes and swishing walk remind me of Eeyore as her head bows from one side to the next. Sometimes we end up at the back door, meaning she needs to go potty. Sometimes it's at her water dish, where her eyes look down at the near-empty bowl and then back to me, back to her bowl, back to me, as if to say, "I'm thirsty, you idiot!" But most times, she wants to join Tony in the garage as he smokes. Baby uses her eyes to move Tony from her spot on the couch. When he stands up or slides over, she steps onto the couch, curling her big body to fit onto one cushion, her head on top of the arm as she looks out the window.

I have never had a pet communicate so fiercely with her eyes.

I prefer her eyes to her horse-like paws that feel more like a hoof than a paw when it lands on the forearm. Once you start petting Baby, she doesn't want you to stop, pawing at your hand the second you stop moving. I fear those hoof-like paws, thinking one day she's going to pounce on me, requiring a life-saving surgery like Mary Ingalls needed when a horse kicked her. I told Tony, "I'm not taking a dishwashing job so you can have surgery."

She uses her snout for booping us, herding us where she wants us. She boops our arms to move it out of her way; she boops our butts if she wants to play. Her snout is like a fifth limb—a surprisingly strong limb—that is more effective than a paw or a bark.

Baby has turned into a miniature horse-sized Kippy. She contorts herself to squeeze between the toilet and the wall; I must contort myself around her to use the toilet. She likes blankets, although she pants when not on the hardwood floor. She loves walking on just-mopped floors too, although she's much ornerier, jumping on the couch as we clean, making sure she makes eye contact with us as she peers over the couch.

And Baby loves Snuggle Time. Except we don't call it Snuggle Time. It's turned into Finger Time.

If Tony buzzes like a bee and then uses his fingers to fly around, Baby's eyes turn crazy, flopping herself around. She pounces and attacks, gnawing on Tony's hand. Baby roots under the blanket to find those fingers that are walking under it. Once she tires of it, she sprawls out under the big picture window in the living room to cool off, booping her way through my sheer curtains first, ending up with one dangled over her head as she dramatically flops to the floor. She reminds me of a cartoon character as her paws struggle to gain traction on my hard floors, running in place before she takes off, unable to put on the brakes as she slides into corners and walls.

Baby doesn't care much for alone time. Which sounds great on paper, but she won't go outside by herself in the summer. She'll only lay down on the deck to chew on sticks if someone is outside with her. Winter is her signature season as she throws around her balls (or a sock she stole from the laundry room), galloping around the yard, rooting in fluffy snow piles. She's already figured out the suitcases, falling into a depression when Tony took JJ to Minneapolis for the weekend. Baby didn't even eat her nightly ice cream cup. She longingly stared out the window, waiting. At lunch time, she sits pretty in front of the door for me, ears back in a hello. If I don't stop long enough to pet her and give her hugs, she shoves her nose into my butt as I walk away.

Her favorite toys are the large floppy plushies, the ones she can toss into the air and catch, the ones that leave the biggest messes when she dismembers them. Yet Baby struggled on her first Christmas, not realizing she had to tear into the wrapping paper to retrieve her present. However, she loved ripping apart the cardboard rolls as I finished off a wrapping paper. Thinking she was invisible, she'd tiptoe into my office and pluck a cardboard roll from the floor, twisting her head just so to make it through the doorway. She'll never know what it's like to nap on the tree skirt as the baubles rotate overhead because she won't fit underneath it.

Baby farts all the time—jumping up and sitting down seems to push her gas out, little audible squeaks, sometimes as loud as a human fart. We never heard Kippy fart, only smelled the noxious stench that lingered long after Kippy left the room. Baby's farts smell just as bad, perhaps more so due to her size. When we walk into the room, it smells like a baby took a dump in her diaper, bringing back memories of emptying the Diaper Genie.

The name Baby fits her well. I console her on those days when everyone is busy. "It's tough being a little puppy, when Papa's got to work, and Momma is writing." She'll sigh with agreement, although her wagging tail gives away her pitiful act. Tony cleans the goop from the corner of her eyes, just like he did with Kippy. I fondly call her Grandpa J, as she stands in the doorway and refuses to move when you need to walk by (Mom would do an excellent impersonation of my Grandpa J leaning in the doorway while she tried to maneuver around him with a handful of plates). Baby doesn't like to be alone, seeks out affection, and even looks sad when people don't notice her when we're out walking. She loves her humans as much as we love our dogs.

Perhaps it's the environment that makes the pet, where nurture triumphs over nature. We created Kippy and now we've created Baby—a needy pet who wants attention and hugs and snuggle time and play time. We'll never own the kind of dog that sits quietly off to the side, a prop for Christmas letters or Trick-or-Treating. We end up with the pet that follows you around or stares at you when you sit. We end up with the hundred-pound dog who jumps on your lap, who turns down a fast-food breakfast sandwich because she prefers homecooked flapjacks instead, who nudges open a door while you're trying to exercise and then sits down in the middle of the room so you can't.

The Dog Whisperer would crucify us.

BARBIE CAR

I always wanted a car just like Barbie.

I eventually bought one, the summer of Covid shutdowns, a bright spot in a bleak national (and global) outlook.

My Barbie car changed my perspective on life.

I wanted a Bug, preferably Jan Brady green, with eyelashes on the headlights. But they didn't make those by the time I bought a convertible. Dad, ever the car connoisseur, suggested an adorable car that screamed Julie: a Miata. With a vintage look and its two-seater design, it was made for Barbie, especially in soul red. I didn't want to mess with a soft top, so upgraded to a hard top, turning my car into a Transformer. Its tiny trunk accentuated my current downsizing attitude and less-is-more philosophy.

All that metal released me from so many pressures, alleviated stress, and freed me from routine.

Driving around aimlessly running silly errands was no longer a nuisance, a time waster on an overly busy day. I felt more energized after driving my Barbie car. My rushed afternoon to-do list faded like cheap construction paper left in the sun. I looked forward to spontaneous errands even during rush hour traffic. It's more time for me to enjoy the sun, the wind in my hair, the heat on my forehead, the stereo surprising me with nostalgic songs (how did I live for so long without the Eighties station on Sirius?). My Barbie car made me present, slowed down my White Rabbit. I never rushed for anything anymore.

Even my tiny trunk challenged me to think differently about purchases, a never-ending learning process that tested my shopping habits. I could fit a case of Coke, two 6-pack bottles of Diet Mt. Dew, a bag of sunflower seeds, and eight bags of groceries inside my miniature trunk. So what if we had to fit it in like puzzle pieces, wondering if the bread would be smashed when we got home (it wasn't). I had no idea that a tiny trunk would prompt me to look at my existence differently.

The first time I drove my red bullet, it released me from the doldrums of the monotony that sustains most of our existence. The little things, like waiting thirteen seconds for the top to open or close, provided me with patience. A no-rush, no-worries attitude that is uncharacteristic of me. Every time I wait for the top to latch into place, I smile with nostalgia as I remember the end scene from the original *A Nightmare on Elm Street*, when Johnny Depp's long red convertible top closes on its own, now painted with Freddy Kruger's sweater colors—dirty red and green. Even my little side mirrors are reminiscent of Barbie's convertibles (at least mine don't fall off with use like hers). The past and the present collide, but not with the shatter they used to. It's as if the car exists unhindered by time, bringing me along for a joyful ride where the past can be present without longing or regret.

And then we adopted Baby, a big dog, who wouldn't disappear inside a car, but sits up like a person. When she was a puppy, she could barely see over the ledge of the door, standing on her hind legs for a better view of her surroundings. Now she reminds me of Barbie's Afghan hound Beauty, perfect posture, her head almost above the windshield. I must look around her now before I can turn.

We go through drive-thrus together, and I take her to the gas station to get my free fountain pop as she waits patiently in the car. Tony drives her in the mornings for their breakfast run; he ends up with free Pup Cups, donut holes, and probably phone numbers from college girls (or the old ladies at McDonald's). Baby stays home on hot summer days, preferring the cool spring and fall temperatures that are just warm enough to drive with the top down.

My Barbie car has become a catalyst for a change in perspective. It gives me something to look forward to every day, those extra minutes in the sunshine, careless moments that need not be rushed or scheduled.

Such freedom has calmed me down. Perhaps sitting so close to the road has grounded me, yet without a roof over my head, it feels as though I'm in the clouds. Worlds have coalesced into the place I am with the place I longed to be. They're one in the same.

And now I have Baby to sit next to me.

FRIENDLY FURRIES

Dogs attract people—at least big, friendly, non-pit-bull dogs. Those with small yippy dogs don't seem to garner the attention that big dog owners do because rarely did anyone comment on Ginger. Maybe we associate such princess furballs with the entitled Paris Hilton or Sharon Osbourne. But Baby attracts everyone.

When we're out on walks, people have stopped their cars in the middle of the road or have pulled over to the curb to tell us, "She's so pretty" or even "He's so handsome."

Baby is pretty. She's fluffy and possesses a friendly visage that overrides her large size. People mistake her for a Saint Bernard, although she isn't brown and white. Her face is much narrower, and her snout is much longer. Only my generation must associate such a dog with Cujo because the last description I would attribute to Cujo, even before they covered him in ketchup and syrup, would be pretty.

People stop us to talk about the dog—drive-thru employees, store patrons, and car washers all ask about her, which then leads to a conversation about their dogs, both alive and dead, or their friends' dogs, or their neighbors' dogs. People without dog connections want to talk to us about their pickup or their lawn or the weather. Funny no one tells us about their cats. No one said much of anything to us when we walked around the neighborhood pre-Baby. Now everyone wants to pet Baby while they say, "She's so pretty." The young and the old, men and women all say, "She's so pretty."

I would have described Ginger as prettier than Baby, but the public must know something I do not.

A comradery exists between dog owners: the friendlier the dog, the friendlier the owners must be. It's like smokers—how a bunch of smoking strangers can shoot the shit for the duration of a cigarette, huddled together within one small outdoor nook that's designated for such social outcasts. An unhealthy socially disapproved activity connects such strangers no matter their differences in age, gender, race, or religion. Dogs have the same effect.

It shouldn't surprise me, as every time I see a dog—a cute one, a nice one, an old one, a well-behaved one—I squeal and want to pet it. But if a pitbull or a rottweiler walks by, my inner Judge Judy criticizes, wondering why people want mean dogs. Yet I suppose those mean dog owners wonder why anyone would want such a skittish rat-looking Chihuahua.

Those constant comments of "She's so pretty" surprise me when I'm by myself since I am not an approachable person. I give off serious bitch vibes with my aloofness and wardrobe. I'm either singing whatever song is playing at the store (the days of mask-wearing meant I could do this without looking insane, but I wore masks much longer than the rest of society, so now it's a habit I struggle to break although I'm not sure I want to stop an activity that brings me joy even if I look crazy as I sing along to Richard Marx while I dig for the freshest loaf of bread) or I'm avoiding interactions, which is easy to do in the age of self-checkouts, self-serve, and order kiosks. My introverted nature thrives when I can shop or eat around people yet never have to interact with any of them, but Baby always draws attention.

Driving my Barbie car also brings attention. I've automatically enrolled in the convertible club whether I want to or not; other convertible drivers give me a half wave or a nod as we pass each other on the street. I attract old men who want to talk about hotrods, as if I have any knowledge of such topics. When Tony drives my Barbie car, he receives comments like "Cool car" and "Awesome car." Yet when I drive my car, women tell me, "Good for you," as if I must have a reason or permission or approval to drive such a car, whereas a man is expected and entitled to such a vehicle.

Combine Baby with my wardrobe and Barbie car and I am as visible as a goat in a candy store.

Women hate to see me glide up next to Tony at Petco. When the unsuspecting girl finds a sudden reason to leave once I arrive, I say, "She wanted to ask you out." Tony blushes ever so slightly. "It's the dog, not me."

Plenty of college girls love the combination of the car and the dog. The donut girls always give Tony free donut holes to give Baby. They give me nothing.

We assume that cute-dog people possess an affability that non-dog owners cannot. One cannot worry about artwork or Persian rugs or crystal vases in the presence of a large dog, especially the kind of breed that looks like it could herd sheep, roll around with kids, or star in a children's book. Such dog owners accept scratches on hardwood floors, scrapes in painted mopboards, and splotchy drool-marked windows. These assumptions make us less neurotic and more adaptable. At least as first impressions.

Dogs provide an icebreaker without pretention. Haughtiness might exist with snobby dog breeds, but Baby isn't one of them with her slightly goofy face that invites affection from strangers. Baby's name is known in the neighborhood while our human ones are not. She attracts all kinds of people no matter education, finances, or politics. All politicians should be forced to own a dog and bring it with them to Congress (maybe then politicians would work together). With the state of current society, such an idea certainly isn't going to worsen it.

Dating apps should exist that focus on our pets. No pictures of the owners, just the pets. The algorithm would match the pets first, then the people. No one would need to catfish anymore because we'd focus on the dog. Baby has given my husband plenty of opportunities to pursue, although as of yet, no woman has asked for his number (so he says).

Tony has always assumed that I get asked out all the time when I'm out and about. I tell him I'm too unapproachable. Only old men compliment me on my Donna Reed wardrobe, ending with "You just don't see women dressing up all that much anymore."

That is until Baby.

On one fountain pop run to my nearest gas station, I threw my hair up into a bun with my metal stick, which I've fondly called my sticky bun since high school. It wasn't even a cute messy bun, but one that was flat on the top with my sides parted down the middle. My eyeliner had smudged in the heat, my sunscreen-infused foundation left greasy residue on my face, and my lipstick had all but vanished. I slipped my feet into my customary high-heeled flipflops, this time a red pair with a low heel. My blue and white strapless sundress made whiter by the dog hair that covered it.

I left Baby in the car with the top down as I ran inside the gas station for my Cherry Coke. Upon my return, a tanned, sunglasses-wearing guy stepped out of his company pickup. "Nice car," he hollered at me from the gas pumps.

I said what I always do: "Thank you." I placed my pop in the car before getting in (it's easier than trying to maneuver into such a low car with a dress, heels, and a pop, with a drink holder that's awkwardly toward the back between the seats).

After a pause, he yelled at me again. "Can I just say you look very beautiful."

I smiled at him as I put on my sunglasses. His voice reminded me of Glenn from *The Walking Dead*, which paired nicely with his crewcut—and probably his age. "Thank you," I said again as I started the car.

I pet Baby's head as she rested her chin on the window ledge, sizing up the interloper, probably wanting to return home to get out of the heat.

"Nice dog. Are you single?"

I stifled my laugh at our probable age discrepancy. "No."

Glenn's doppelganger shook his head. "Fuck my life."

He should get a dog.

HELLO, SHAKESPEARE: AN EPILOGUE

A cat person can't end a memoir on a dog chapter. Enter Shakespeare, a black and white long-haired kitten who meowed at me from a Humane Society cage. The black of his nose looks painted on, the kind drawn on a human's nose for Halloween, smudged slightly to the left, like he moved while it was still being drawn. If the smudge had been lower, he would look like Mr. Pitt from *Seinfeld*, after the incident with the ink.

As expected, Shakespeare howled in his backpack carrier, both from the shelter and to the vet.

Tony is not my competition for Shakespeare's attention—it's Baby, whom Shakespeare seeks upon waking. Baby took a few days to warm up to her new doll, mothering it like an American Doll that was designed for her, for Baby's and Shakespeare's fur blends together. Shakespeare's whole body is pushed around by Baby's snout, and he's cleaned daily with Baby's wet tongue. I should have named him Gremlin, for that's what Shakespeare looks like after contact with Baby's tongue—not the Gizmo variety, but the kind of Gremlin that develops when you feed them after midnight.

The adjustment period was not the ease of which we experienced with Ginger and Kippy, an easy transition I realize now probably doesn't happen all that often. We had to constantly monitor Baby for fear she would squash Shakespeare with her dinosaur feet. Baby acted true to toddler form—the older child who had long outgrown baby toys now taking kitten toys and destroying them. When I finally got the children settled, with Shakespeare napping on my lap while I sat on the chaise in the library, Baby sat next to me, staring.

I sighed. I didn't want to get up to have to let her out to go potty. "What do you want?"

Baby looked at me, then at Shakespeare, then back to me, then at Shakespeare, then at me again. I laughed and petted her head. "I bet you do want this kitty." But for what? Smother it and bury it in the backyard? Snatch it from my lap so it could sit in her lap? Or move the cat so Baby could sit in my lap?

Although the first night went smoothly, the next night I ended up on the couch with Shakespeare while I shut Baby in our bedroom. The third night, Tony got up with them at four in the morning. They have since regulated themselves, everybody sleeping through the night, more or less, except when Shakespeare turns into Mr. Snuggles and curls up under our chins at two in the morning (I wish we could put Shakespeare to bed downstairs, but with Baby that's not possible).

As a kitten, when Shakespeare woke from a nap, he sat in the hallway and meowed a meow that was ten times his body size. He didn't seem to care who responded—me, Tony, JJ, or Baby—but was just in need of somebody, like a baby in a crib. Currently I set his food on the counter because Baby now wants to eat pet food, any kind, all the time. Shakespeare doesn't always want his food when he meows. Sometimes he wants to cuddle, sometimes he wants to play, sometimes he wants to be held, and well, sometimes we don't know what he wants. I've had to stop writing this chapter twice so far, as he has meowed at my feet, purring away, wanting me to hold him.

I don't mind. The neediest cat picked me. Or I picked the neediest cat.

I don't regret the itchy chest and neck that plagues me every day. I ignore the impulse to scratch. Fancy Feast rose in price again—the last cans I bought for Kippy cost 76 cents. In just 18 months, they are now 88 cents. I gladly lug kitty litter in my cart again. Shakespeare adores little colored springs that he bats around the floor, carrying in his teeth to move them out of corners, and then hurtling them under the refrigerator or the couch. I set a small bowl of food next to his bed on the trunk in my office, out of Baby's reach, in case Shakespeare desires a midday snack. My writing office, complete with a cat again.

Of course there are those brief moments of buyer's remorse, especially when Shakespeare steps in his own poop and leaves poopy pawprints through the house, or when he's chewing on computer charger cords as I pray he doesn't end up like the cat in *National Lampoon's Christmas Vacation*. But those moments don't last, just those passing panics that every new parent experiences, when the momentary stress overrides the joy of a new baby (the human variety).

It passes as soon as Shakespeare meows or purrs or does his two-step and crazy side leap as he plays. Or better yet, the little purr-squeak that emits from his mouth every time he jumps down, stretches, or plops on his side.

Shakespeare has added even more laughter to the household: he growls at anyone who comes between him and his piece of Chick-fil-A or roast beef and he dives off the couch onto Baby with his front paws out like Superman. He runs to the door when we ask, "You want to go outside?" barreling past Baby so he can stalk the birds eating under my tree. Shakespeare looks like a prince as he rides in his pink stroller on Baby's walks—he knows what going for a walk means and jumps in his stroller.

We refer to Shakespeare and Baby as The Kids—they're together in my small entryway by the back door, they run up and down the stairs no matter how many times I tell them not to play on the steps, they nap together—Shakespeare curls up next to Baby's mouth. They watch television together at night too. When their roughhousing carries on too long, I say, "Stop," to which they both look at me with the same innocent face. The chaos they create might look cringeworthy for non-pet people, the kind who think *glad it's not me*, the same thoughts we think when we see parents trying to herd their four children into a car. Yet there's joy in that chaos, even as you swear when you almost trip as Baby refuses to move and Shakespeare lets out a yelp because someone stepped on his paw. My home feels more alive, its spirit refreshed as Baby chews on a cat toy with big eyes as she awaits the "Give me that" and Shakespeare practices his ten-yard dash back and forth underneath my living room curtains, a constant flutter of sheers as if the window was open.

As much as I love Baby, and dogs in general, a cat is the frosting on the cupcake. The little paws reaching to play with the whisps of hair that dangle near my face. The purring as I cuddle him to my chest. The tiny oohs that escape his mouth as he re-positions himself while he sleeps. The squeaky meows as he sits and stares at me as I wonder what it is he's saying.

Now if only I could get Shakespeare to enjoy car rides.

without a dog what a dog can do for a household. Coming home at lunchtime is one of my favorite times of day—you sit so pretty and stare into my eyes as I pet you, even if I feel I'm about ready to pee my pants. I forgot the happiness in giving dogs hugs. Now can we figure out a way to stop the drooling?

To Shakespeare—aka Mr. Snuggles. You are the perfect cat for a writer, as you plop on my desk, knocking over my pink pen cup, sprawling out as your paws whack my keyboard. Your little squeaks and purrs delight me. Thank you for no longer playing Alien in the middle of the night. If you ever lose your Woobie, I will be just as devastated as you. You are the reason cat people exist.

MEET THE AUTHOR

Julie Ann is the author of two self-published memoirs—and understands why Prince and Madonna went through a phase of refusing to perform their first singles. A teacher of literature and writing at both college and high school levels, she squeezes in as much reading and writing as possible, then berates herself when she's lazy. She created Book Smart Pop-Up in 2023 in the hopes we all get a little bit smarter through books while avoiding algorithms on our phones. She lives in the Midwest with her ex-husband, their college-aged son, a dog the size of a pony, and a cat who in a past life was an engineer.

www.ingramcontent.com/pod-product-compliance
Lightning Source LLC
Chambersburg PA
CBHW021214130626
46554CB00004B/1223